THE PRESENCE-DRIVEN LEADER

THE PRESENCE-DRIVEN LEADER

Lead With Presence, Not Position

Victor Simmons

Copyright © 2026 by Victor Simmons.

All rights reserved. No part of this book may be reproduced in any written, electronic, or recorded form or photocopied without written permission from the publisher or author. If you would like permission to use material from the book (other than for review purposes), please contact the publisher. Thank you for your support of the author's rights.

To purchase books in bulk, please contact the publisher.

Mynd Matters Publishing
2690 Cobb Parkway SE
Ste A5-375
Smyrna, GA 30080
www.myndmatterspublishing.com

ISBN: 978-1-963874-79-2 (pbk)
ISBN: 978-1-963874-80-8 (hdcv)
e-ISBN: 978-1-963874-81-5

FIRST EDITION

*To my ancestors, my great-granddad,
my granddad, and my dad, and to my Indio Rajah
teammates, each of whom forged a part of the leader
I am today.*

CONTENTS

FOREWORD
9

INTRODUCTION
13

Chapter 1
What is Presence-Driven Leadership?
21

Chapter 2
The Inner Work: Self-Awareness & Reflection
31

Chapter 3
Coaching Through Challenges
43

Chapter 4
Influence Without Authority
57

Chapter 5
Leading With Conviction
73

Chapter 6
Real World Leadership Lessons
85

Chapter 7
Building Team Culture Without Titles
97

Chapter 8
Leading Through Crisis and Change
109

Chapter 9
Presence in Today's Workplace
121

Chapter 10
Tools for Immediate Application
133

Chapter 11
Being a Presence-Driven Leader
147

ACKNOWLEDGMENTS
155

ABOUT THE AUTHOR
159

GLOSSARY
161

RESOURCES AND REFERENCES
165

FOREWORD

Victor Simmons joined The Westin Mission Hills Resort & Spa as Director of Human Resources about three weeks before I arrived as General Manager. What I encountered was a leader who had already begun building the relationships and trust that would prove essential during one of the most challenging periods in hospitality history.

Our relationship developed quickly because we were in immediate agreement about a fundamental principle: everyone on our team was more important than we were. That shared commitment to servant leadership became the foundation of everything we built together.

The real estate market crash of 2008 hit our industry hard, and the years that followed tested every principle of leadership we claimed to believe in. As General Manager, I had to make difficult strategic decisions about hiring freezes and being extremely selective about backfilling positions. But Victor's role was equally critical: he had to help implement those decisions while preserving the dignity and humanity of our team members.

During those difficult times, our competitor hotels were laying off 30, 40, and 50 people at a time. While our numbers were lower due to proactive workforce planning, each elimination was still painful. What distinguished our approach was how we treated people during the process. Victor ensured that even in the midst of position eliminations, we showed genuine care and respect for those affected. That's presence-driven leadership under the most difficult circumstances imaginable.

While navigating crisis, Victor and his HR team simultaneously worked to strengthen the organization we were fighting to preserve. Victor's leadership training and education at all levels transformed our property. Our associate engagement scores went from bottom quartile to top 10 in the company. Building that culture made us one of the fastest performing assets in the company across all metrics.

Most senior leadership wanted to know what we did. Victor became a resource for the change that could make properties more profitable and union tough. His approach to developing leaders at every level created measurable business results alongside cultural transformation.

Victor became our property service culture trainer and achieved 90% participation in rolling out Starwood's service culture training resort-wide. That level of engagement during a period of organizational stress doesn't happen by accident. It happens when people trust the leader and believe in the principles the leader teaches.

One initiative in particular demonstrated Victor's strategic thinking and relationship-based influence. He implemented a Six Sigma best practice around employee cafeteria charges that was unheard of in our company at the time. Through preemptive focus groups and careful framing, he achieved buy-in with minimal pushback while maintaining high employee satisfaction scores. That's the kind of leadership that builds trust even when making unpopular changes.

What you'll find in *The Presence-Driven Leader* is exactly what I witnessed Victor demonstrate during both crisis and stability: leadership that doesn't rely on position or authority, but on authentic relationships, genuine care for people's development, and unwavering commitment to doing what's right even when it's difficult.

The hospitality industry, and business in general, needs more leaders who understand that their job isn't just to execute strategy, but to do so in ways that preserve human dignity and build organizational strength simultaneously. Victor doesn't just understand this intellectually. He proved it works during some of the toughest years our industry has faced, delivering both cultural transformation and business results that made other properties want to replicate our approach.

This book provides a practical framework that any leader can use, regardless of their industry or level of authority. The Coach-Influence-Conviction approach isn't theory. It's the distillation of lessons learned through decades of leadership experience, including navigating crisis while maintaining culture and caring for people even during necessary workforce reductions.

If you're looking for leadership wisdom that's been tested under real pressure and delivered measurable results, not just during good times, you'll find it here. If you want to understand how to build influence and develop others while navigating difficult organizational realities, Victor shows you how. And if you believe that leadership should be about treating people with dignity regardless of circumstances while achieving business outcomes that make your organization a model for others, you'll recognize a kindred spirit in these pages.

I've seen Victor's leadership approach transform organizational performance during one of the most demanding periods in hospitality history. Now he's giving you the framework to apply these same principles in your own context, whether you're facing crisis or building for growth.

Ken Pilgrim
Former General Manager
The Westin Mission Hills Resort & Spa

INTRODUCTION

Here's what most people don't understand about leadership: It's not the title on your LinkedIn profile that moves people to action. It's not the corner office or the executive parking space. It's something far more fundamental and far more powerful. It's your presence.

There's a photograph on the wall that sits over my shoulder that changed my life. Three men stand together, spanning nearly a century of leadership—my great-grandfather Bill in the center, my grandfather Willie Fate on the left, and my father Lee on the right. I never met the man in the middle, but his legacy shaped everything I've become as a leader.

Position gets you in the room. Presence keeps you there—and makes people want to listen when you speak. I've seen this truth play out in boardrooms and break rooms, in crisis moments and quiet conversations. The leaders who create lasting change, who build cultures that thrive, who develop other leaders—they all share one thing in common: they understand that influence flows from who you are, not what you're called.

This book is about that understanding. It's about learning to lead with presence, not position. And it's about the practical framework that can transform how you show up as a leader, regardless of your title.

The Legacy of Leadership in My Family

The story begins with Bill Simmons, my great-grandfather, whom I never met but whose influence ripples through my leadership today. Bill was a sharecropper by day and, as family legend tells it, one of the most prolific moonshiners Conecuh County, Alabama had ever seen. Moonshining was what really helped pay the bills at the farm.

Bill raised my father and a large number of siblings and cousins. He taught my father how to drive a truck when he could barely see over the dashboard, showed him how to farm the land, and as my father would say, taught him to "work his tail off." Bill taught him that leadership wasn't just about hard work; it was about having the discipline to do what needed to be done while maintaining the confidence and communication skills to hold your own with anyone, regardless of their position. My father grew up on that farm, learning from Bill. But midway through high school, my grandfather Willie Fate Simmons, who had been working in Akron, Ohio, reached out and invited my father to join him there. That moment opened up an entirely new chapter in my father's life.

While the legacy of hard work and entrepreneurship may have begun with Bill Simmons, the leadership story I carry forward truly begins with my grandfather, Willie Fate.

Grandad was the kind of man who didn't wait for opportunity to knock. He worked three jobs for over 30 years—cook in the Navy Reserve, head maître d' in the executive lounge for Firestone Tires, and waiter in room service at the Mayflower Hotel. Think about what that must have been like for him, starting out in Alabama in

1915, migrating to Akron, Ohio, and navigating life in the late 1930s through the 1960s.

He would work a shift, change uniforms, work another, then do it one more time. What struck me, even as a young boy, was that he never seemed tired. He had to have been exhausted, yet he still found time to laugh, to smile, and to treat every single person he encountered with dignity. He would heap praise on them, too.

"How's it going, Willie!" people would say, and Grandad would respond, "I'm doing real good now that I see you!" He did this with everyone, even folks who weren't reciprocating the courtesy.

His philosophy was simple: "You get more with honey than you do with vinegar."

People paid attention when Grandad spoke, not because he raised his voice but because they didn't want to disappoint him. He made friends easily and earned their respect through how he carried himself, not only by what he said.

After working those three jobs for 30 years, he started his own successful catering business. With an eighth-grade education and a whole lot of self-taught lessons, he even taught himself French and Spanish from old records. The same man who never made it to high school was now serving and hobnobbing with local socialites and executives at events across the city. People tripped over themselves to be around Willie Fate Simmons.

His life wasn't about making a living. It was about pride in what he did, excellence in how he did it, and the legacy he forged.

It was on the shoulders of these two men that my father, Lee F. Simmons came into being. He didn't just make history because he was the first Black steward on Air Force One. To our family, his accomplishments are remembered to this day because he was the pillar of integrity, conviction, of hard work, and quiet excellence. My father was so well loved by friends, family and quite frankly, people who met him within minutes became immediate fans.

He started during the Kennedy administration by a stroke of luck—being in the right place at the right time, but more importantly, being prepared. When a crew member was sick, my father had the required training hours and could fill in on missions. He quickly connected with the pilots and was officially transferred during the Johnson administration. He went on to become Chief Steward under Nixon and continued through the Ford administration.

President Ford was so taken by my father's humility, professionalism, and uncanny ability to foster relationships that when Ford lost his reelection, he asked my father to come work for him as his staff assistant. My father went from the struggles of a farm in Alabama to triumph in the inner circle of Air Force One. Not because he chased titles, but because he moved with humility, servant leadership, and purpose.

Despite missions like the first presidential trips to China and Russia, his career wasn't portrayed as glamorous in our household. It was purposeful. It was about service.

Don't get me wrong. It wasn't easy growing up in a military-run household. As the oldest son with two sisters, I learned early that *how* you do your work matters just as much as what you do. I learned the importance of showing up and being properly prepared when you do, no matter what it takes. I learned humility, how to serve those who count on you, and how to use the right amount of honey or vinegar when needed.

Three generations. One legacy. Leadership isn't about volume. It's not about titles. It's about consistency, humility, and how you treat people.

As I carried my family's legacy forward, I needed to discover my own leadership fire. That discovery came during my senior year at Indio High School in the 1982 California Interscholastic Federation (CIF) championship game against powerhouse Ganesha High.

We were underdogs in every sense. They were stronger, faster, and had us down 20-0 by the start of the fourth quarter. Most teams would have accepted defeat. But we didn't. We had come from behind before in four critical games leading to this moment, never giving up. And on this night, before a sold-out crowd, we clawed our way back and won 21-20.

That experience changed everything for me. I learned that grit beats talent, that heart matters more than hype, and that no matter how far behind you are, it's never too late for a comeback. I wore that championship ring for years as a daily reminder that adversity isn't an obstacle—it's the proving ground for leadership.

Today, I wear my youngest son's wrestling team championship ring. His team won state titles three years in a row. Considering what he and I went through from his junior to senior year, navigating my divorce while he struggled with grades and choices that concerned me, that third championship meant everything. In his final match against his cross-town rival, the grudge match of his entire high school career, he won in the final seconds, securing the team's third consecutive CIF title. When it came time to order his ring, I told him he needed to pay for half because I was buying one for myself. On mine, where you'd normally see the weight class, it says 'Dad.' I wear it with pride, not just for him, but for every person I coach, mentor, and lead who refuses to settle when life gets hard.

These experiences are why I don't like being told "no." When I hear "no," I feel it in my bones. Not because I'm stubborn, but because

I believe that where others see walls, leaders find doors. That mindset has shaped how I coach and lead others.

• • • •

The ultimate test of leading with presence came in 2020, but the journey began years earlier. In 2011, I stepped away from hospitality to run my own consulting firm. I loved the freedom, but I missed the energy of a team. After a long and challenging eighteen months, I found an HR leadership role with Wyndham Hotels.

Within three years at Wyndham, I rose from HR Director to Area Director. After another three years, I was promoted to the corporate offices as Director of Diversity & Inclusion. Then, in April 2020, my role was eliminated during the pandemic.

It was a tough blow, especially when the entire industry was shutting down. But even in the middle of global lockdowns, while most of the industry remained closed, I landed a first-time corporate Vice President role at Atelier Ace, a creative hotel brand. How? Not because of my previous titles or connections, but because of how I showed up during the interview process. I demonstrated presence—the ability to stay grounded, lead with authenticity, and bring value regardless of circumstances.

My father once told me about a time when he was young. Bill bought a truck and told him he'd be driving it home from the dealership ninety miles away. My father had never driven before and was terrified. Bill simply said, "Lee, if you never try, you will never know if you can do this. You have to start someday." After a brief lesson, my father drove that manual transmission truck all the way home, with Bill encouraging him the entire six-hour journey. That experience taught my father to start things he'd never done before, and it always made an impression on me.

That moment reinforced what I already knew from watching Bill teach my father to drive when he was terrified, my grandfather work three jobs with dignity, my father serve presidents with humility, and my own championship comeback: You don't have to wait for ideal circumstances to lead. You lead with presence, no matter the storm.

These experiences taught me that leadership is not inherited—it's developed. It's not about waiting for the perfect role or the right title. It's about cultivating the presence that makes people want to follow you, trust you, and grow under your influence.

In every boardroom, every coaching session, every decision I make, I carry my family legacy forward. More importantly, I've developed a practical framework that any leader can use to develop their own presence-driven leadership approach.

This book is organized around three core elements that transform positional leaders into presence-driven leaders: Coach, Influence, and Conviction. You'll learn how to coach through challenges rather than simply manage problems, how to influence without relying on authority, and how to lead with conviction while maintaining the humility that draws people to you.

You'll discover real-world strategies I've used in hospitality, consulting, and corporate environments—from building authentic relationships that strengthen organizational culture to navigating DEI resistance with courage and wisdom. You'll see how presence-driven leadership applies whether you're managing a team of five or leading an organization of thousands.

Most importantly, you'll walk away with practical tools you can implement immediately. Because leadership development isn't a someday goal—it's a today opportunity.

The question isn't whether you have what it takes to lead. The question is: Are you ready to lead with presence rather than position?

Your people are waiting for you to show up. Not as the person your title says you should be, but as the leader your presence reveals you can become.

The journey starts now.

CHAPTER 1

What is Presence-Driven Leadership?

Walk into any organization today and you'll witness a fundamental divide in how people approach leadership. Some leaders operate from their position and title, while others lead from authentic presence and earned respect. Research consistently shows that leaders who are self-aware about their style and can articulate their approach are more effective at building trust, driving performance, and creating positive organizational cultures. Yet, despite decades of leadership development programs, the majority of the U.S. workforce (77%) is not engaged at work, and the connection between strong leadership and employee engagement is well documented (Washington, DC: Gallup, 2023).

Some leaders operate from their title. They reference their position in conversations, rely on organizational charts to get things done, and measure their success by the authority they wield. When they speak, people listen because they have to.

Others lead from something deeper. When they enter a room, the energy shifts. People lean in when they talk, seek their input on decisions, and follow their lead even when they're not officially in charge. Their influence extends far beyond their job description, and their impact lasts long after they've moved on to new roles.

The difference between these two leaders isn't their experience, education, or industry knowledge. It's their understanding of a fundamental truth: Position is temporary, but presence is portable.

This chapter is about making the shift from the first type of leader to the second. It's about understanding what presence-driven leadership really means, why it matters more than ever in today's workplace, and how you can begin developing it regardless of your current role.

Most leadership development focuses on what to do when you get the promotion, the corner office, or the bigger team. We're taught to think of leadership as a destination rather than a practice. This creates what I call the positional leadership trap: the belief that influence comes from hierarchy and that leadership is something you do after you get the title.

Positional leaders operate from a scarcity mindset. They hoard information because knowledge equals power. They make decisions in isolation because consultation might undermine their authority. They focus on being right rather than being effective because their credibility feels tied to their infallibility.

Here's the problem: This approach worked when careers were predictable, organizational structures were stable, and change happened slowly. But today's workplace demands something entirely different.

Consider Sarah, a director I coached at a mid-sized technology company. She had been promoted quickly based on her technical expertise and was struggling to get her team to execute on strategic initiatives. In our first conversation, she said, "I don't understand why they won't just do what I tell them. I'm their boss."

Sarah was trapped in positional thinking. She believed her title should automatically trigger compliance, but her team had learned to do only the minimum required to avoid conflict. They weren't engaged, they weren't innovative, and they certainly weren't developing into future leaders themselves.

The shift began when Sarah realized that her team's lack of engagement wasn't a reflection of their competence—it was feedback about her leadership approach. Once she started leading with presence rather than position, everything changed. But we'll return to Sarah's transformation later in this chapter.

Defining Presence-Driven Leadership

Presence-driven leadership is the ability to influence, inspire, and develop others through who you are rather than what you're called. It's leadership that travels with you from role to role, team to team, and organization to organization.

When you lead with presence, people follow you because they want to, not because they must. They trust your judgment because you've demonstrated wisdom, not because your opinion carries more weight on the organizational chart. They come to you with problems because you've shown the ability to coach them toward solutions, not because you have the authority to mandate fixes.

Presence-driven leadership has four core characteristics:

1. **Authenticity Over Image Management:** Presence-driven leaders show up as their genuine selves rather than performing a version of what they think leadership should look like. They acknowledge what they don't know, admit

their mistakes, and lead from their strengths while openly addressing their development areas.

2. **Service Over Self-Interest**: These leaders measure success by others' growth and achievement. They ask, "How can I help you succeed?" before they ask, "What can you do for me?" Their primary focus is on developing people and removing obstacles that prevent their teams from doing their best work.

3. **Influence Over Authority**: Rather than relying on their position to get things done, presence-driven leaders build credibility through consistent actions, clear communication, and demonstrated competence. They understand that sustainable influence must be earned continuously, not granted once.

4. **Values Over Convenience**: When decisions get difficult, presence-driven leaders default to their core values rather than the path of least resistance. They're willing to have hard conversations, make unpopular choices, and stand firm on principles even when it would be easier to compromise.

Presence-driven leadership builds on the foundation of servant leadership, a concept developed by Robert Greenleaf. This leadership style turns traditional leadership hierarchy upside down. Instead of accumulating and expecting others to serve them, servant leaders use their influence to serve others' growth and success.

Presence-driven leadership takes servant leadership a step further. While servant leadership focuses on the leader's orientation toward others, presence-driven leadership emphasizes the leader's orientation toward themselves as well as others. You cannot authentically serve others until you clearly understand who you are, what you value, and how you show up in the world.

This self-awareness doesn't lead to self-absorption. Instead, it creates the foundation for genuine service. When you're clear about your own strengths, blind spots, and motivations, you can engage with others from a place of confidence rather than defensiveness. You can focus on their development rather than your own insecurities.

My grandfather Willie Fate embodied this perfectly. His three jobs required him to serve others all day long, but his ability to do so with joy and dignity came from his clear sense of who he was and what he valued. He never confused his role with his identity, which allowed him to bring his full presence to every interaction.

Why Organizations Need This Shift Now

The workplace has fundamentally changed, but many leadership approaches haven't kept pace. Consider these realities:

Flatter Organizational Structures: Many companies have eliminated middle management layers, meaning leaders must influence across levels and departments without formal authority over key stakeholders.

Remote and Hybrid Work: When face-to-face interaction is limited, leaders can't rely on physical presence or informal relationship-building to create influence. Their leadership must translate through digital communication and virtual collaboration.

Generational Expectations: Younger employees expect transparency, development opportunities, and meaningful work. They're less likely to accept "because I said so" as sufficient reasoning and more likely to leave organizations where they don't feel valued or developed.

Rapid Change: The pace of business change means that yesterday's expertise may be less relevant today. Leaders must be comfortable with uncertainty and able to learn alongside their teams rather than always having the answers.

Knowledge Work Complexity: Many roles require creativity, problem-solving, and collaboration that can't be managed through traditional command-and-control methods. These outcomes require engagement and ownership that only comes from intrinsic motivation.

Research from Gallup consistently shows that employee engagement globally hovers around 20-23%, meaning the majority of people (62%) are not engaged or are actively disengaged (15%) and just going through the motions (Gallup, 2024). This isn't a performance problem—it's a leadership problem, and it can't be solved by better processes or clearer job descriptions. It requires leaders who can connect with people at a human level and inspire them to bring their best effort to work.

The Presence-Driven Leadership Assessment

Before we go further, let's establish your starting point. This assessment will help you understand your current leadership approach and identify areas for development. For each statement below, rate yourself on a scale of 1-5, where one is "Never" and five is "Always."

Authenticity Indicators:
- I admit when I don't know something, rather than trying to appear knowledgeable

- I acknowledge my mistakes quickly and focus on solutions
- I ask for feedback about my leadership and genuinely consider what I hear
- People tell me I'm the same person in meetings as I am in casual conversations

Service Indicators:
- I regularly ask team members how I can help them succeed
- I spend more time developing others than promoting my own achievements
- I remove obstacles for my team even when it requires extra effort from me
- I celebrate others' successes as enthusiastically as my own

Influence Indicators:
- People seek my input on decisions even when I'm not the decision-maker
- I can get things done through people who don't report to me
- My ideas get implemented because of their merit, not my position
- I can change minds through discussion rather than directive

Values Indicators:
- I can clearly articulate what I stand for as a leader
- I make consistent decisions even when circumstances change
- I'm willing to have difficult conversations when values are at stake
- People know what to expect from me regardless of the situation

> ### SCORING
> - **64-80:** You're already leading with strong presence. This book will help you refine and expand your approach.
> - **48-63:** You have a solid foundation, but there remains a significant opportunity to develop your presence-driven leadership.
> - **32-47:** You're likely relying heavily on position and would benefit from fundamental shifts in approach.
> - **Below 32:** You have tremendous growth potential. This book will provide the framework for transformation.

Sarah's Transformation

Remember Sarah, the technology director who couldn't understand why her team wouldn't simply execute her directives? Here's how her transformation unfolded.

First, Sarah had to let go of the belief that her title should generate automatic compliance. This was hard because her promotion had validated her technical skills, and she feared that admitting uncertainty would undermine her credibility.

We started with authenticity. In her next team meeting, instead of presenting a fully formed strategy and expecting implementation, Sarah said, "I've been thinking about our Q3 priorities, but I want to hear your perspectives before we finalize anything. What challenges are you seeing that I might be missing?"

The conversation that followed was unlike any her team had experienced. They shared insights about customer pain points she hadn't considered, identified resource constraints that would affect timelines, and proposed solutions she wouldn't have thought of alone.

Next, we worked on service orientation. Sarah began having weekly one-on-one conversations with each team member focused entirely on their development and success. She asked questions like, "What part of your role energizes you most?" and "What skills would you like to develop this quarter?" She then used these insights to adjust project assignments and create growth opportunities.

The influence shift happened naturally. As Sarah became more authentic and service-oriented, people started coming to her with ideas and concerns. They sought her input on decisions outside her direct authority. Other department heads began including her in strategic conversations because her team's engagement and performance had become noticeably stronger.

Eighteen months later, Sarah's team had the highest employee satisfaction scores in the company. Their project delivery had improved by 25%, and three team members had been promoted to leadership roles in other departments. Sarah herself was promoted to VP, but more importantly, she had discovered a leadership approach that would serve her throughout her career.

The Journey Ahead

Developing presence-driven leadership isn't about perfecting a set of techniques. It's about committing to ongoing growth in four key areas: self-awareness, coaching ability, influence skills, and values-based decision-making.

The framework we'll explore in the coming chapters—Coach, Influence, Conviction—provides the practical structure for this development. But remember, presence-driven leadership is ultimately about who you are, not what you do. The techniques and strategies matter, but they must be grounded in genuine commitment to serving others and leading from your authentic self.

Every leader has a choice in every interaction: Will you lead from your position or your presence? Will you rely on your title or your character? Will you focus on compliance or commitment?

Your answers to these questions don't just determine your effectiveness as a leader. They determine the kind of workplace culture you create, the type of people you develop, and the legacy you leave behind.

The good news? You can begin leading with presence immediately, regardless of your current role. You don't need permission, a promotion, or a perfect plan. You just need the commitment to show up differently.

Your team is waiting. Your organization needs it and your future leadership effectiveness depends on it.

The journey starts with understanding who you are beneath the title. That's where we're headed next.

CHAPTER 2

The Inner Work: Self-Awareness & Reflection

"Know thyself" was inscribed at the Temple of Apollo at Delphi over 2,400 years ago, yet it remains the most challenging and essential work any leader will ever do. You cannot lead others effectively until you understand who you are, what drives you, and how you show up in the world.

Rather than being about navel-gazing or endless self-analysis, it's about developing the self-awareness that allows you to lead from a place of authenticity rather than performance, strength rather than insecurity, and purpose rather than position.

Every presence-driven leader I've worked with has done this inner work. They've confronted their blind spots, clarified their values, and learned to manage their triggers. They understand that leadership development starts with self-development, and they've committed to the ongoing process of growth and reflection.

This chapter will guide you through that same journey. You'll discover tools for honest self-assessment, learn how to identify and address your leadership blind spots, and develop the reflective practices that will accelerate your growth as a leader.

The Foundation of Presence-Driven Leadership

Self-awareness is the bedrock of presence-driven leadership. When you're clear about your strengths, weaknesses, values, and motivations, you can show up authentically in any situation. You're not performing a version of leadership you think people expect—you're leading from who you genuinely are.

Research in neuroscience shows that self-aware leaders have better emotional regulation, make more thoughtful decisions, and build stronger relationships with their teams (Goleman, 1998). A study by organizational psychologist Tasha Eurich found that while 95% of people think they're self-aware, only 10-15% actually are (Eurich 2017). This gap between perception and reality creates significant challenges for leaders who believe they understand themselves better than they actually do.

The leaders who develop genuine self-awareness share several characteristics:

They seek feedback actively rather than defensively. Instead of waiting for annual reviews or formal assessments, they regularly ask colleagues, team members, and supervisors for input about their leadership effectiveness.

They can articulate their values clearly and live them consistently. They don't just know what they believe in—they can explain why those values matter and demonstrate them through their actions, especially when it's difficult.

They understand their emotional triggers and have strategies for managing them. They recognize what situations, people, or circumstances tend to provoke strong reactions, and they've developed healthy ways to respond rather than react.

They know their strengths and leverage them while addressing their development areas. They're realistic about what they do well and what they need to improve, and they're intentional about both maximizing their strengths and closing their gaps.

The self-awareness work we're discussing directly correlates to specific quadrants of emotional intelligence, and research shows clear connections between these capabilities and leadership success.

Daniel Goleman's emotional intelligence framework identifies four core areas. The inner work of presence-driven leadership strengthens two of them in particular:

Self-Awareness (Internal Focus): This includes recognizing your emotions, understanding your triggers, and knowing your strengths and limitations. Research by the Center for Creative Leadership found that executives who demonstrate higher self-awareness—measured by alignment between their self-ratings and how others rate them—tend to receive higher leadership performance ratings and are significantly less likely to experience career derailment (Center for Creative Leadership, "Understanding Your 360 Results").

Self-Management (Internal Focus): This involves controlling disruptive emotions, adapting to change, and maintaining standards of honesty and integrity. Research by TalentSmart found that 90% of top performers are high in emotional intelligence, with EQ being the strongest predictor of performance, explaining 58% of success across all types of jobs (Bradberry & Greaves, *Emotional Intelligence 2.0*)."

Leaders who excel in these internally focused areas of emotional intelligence demonstrate measurably better outcomes. Research by the Korn Ferry Institute analyzed nearly 7,000 professionals at 486 publicly traded companies and found that companies with higher rates of return consistently employed professionals who exhibited higher levels of self-awareness. Poorly performing companies had 20% more leadership blind spots than financially strong companies (Korn Ferry Institute, *A Better Return on Self-Awareness*).

The work you'll do in this chapter—identifying values, managing triggers, and building reflection practices—directly develops these high-impact emotional intelligence capabilities.

Understanding Your Leadership Blind Spots

Blind spots are the areas where our self-perception doesn't match reality. They're called blind spots because, by definition, we can't see them ourselves. They require an external perspective to identify and ongoing attention to address. Common leadership blind spots include:

The Communication Gap: You believe you're being clear and direct, but others experience you as confusing or harsh. Or you think you're being supportive and encouraging, but your team feels micromanaged.

The Impact Disconnect: You intend to be helpful and collaborative, but others perceive you as controlling or intrusive. Your desire to add value comes across as a lack of trust in their capabilities.

The Consistency Challenge: You believe you treat everyone fairly, but certain team members feel you have favorites. Your attempts to individualize your approach are seen as inconsistent standards.

The Delegation Dilemma: You think you're empowering your team by staying involved, but they feel you're not truly delegating. Your desire to support is experienced as hovering.

The Feedback Filter: You believe you're open to input, but others see you as defensive or dismissive. Your questions, intended to understand, are perceived as challenges to their credibility.

Consider Alex, a regional manager I coached who was surprised to learn that his team found him intimidating. Alex saw himself as passionate and direct—qualities that had served him well in his technical roles. But as a leader, his intensity was causing people to withhold ideas and concerns. They were afraid of his reaction to problems or disagreements.

The breakthrough came when Alex realized that his intention to show enthusiasm was being interpreted as impatience with anything less than perfection. Once he understood the gap, he was able to adjust his approach without losing his natural energy and drive.

Identifying Your Core Values

Values are the principles that guide your decisions and actions, especially when you're under pressure or facing difficult choices. They're not aspirational statements about who you want to be—they're accurate descriptions of what truly matters to you.

Many leaders can recite their organization's values or list qualities they admire, but they struggle to identify their own core values. This clarity is essential for presence-driven leadership because your values serve as your decision-making compass.

The Values Discovery Process

Step 1: Peak Experience Analysis: Think about three times in your life when you felt most proud, fulfilled, and authentic. These don't have to be work-related. What values were you honoring in those moments? What principles were you living out?

Step 2: Frustration Analysis: Identify three situations that made you most angry or frustrated in the past year. What values were being violated in those moments? Often, our strongest negative reactions point to our deepest-held values.

Step 3: Decision Analysis: Recall three difficult decisions you've made in the past two years. What principles guided your choices? What values helped you decide when the options were all challenging?

Step 4: Values Prioritization: From your analysis, create a list of 8-10 values that emerged consistently. Then force-rank them. If you had to choose between two of these values in a difficult situation, which would take priority?

Your top five values become your leadership compass. They should guide how you make decisions, communicate with others, and approach challenging situations.

Managing Your Emotional Triggers

Every leader has emotional triggers—situations, behaviors, or comments that provoke strong reactions. The key to presence-driven leadership isn't eliminating these triggers (that's impossible), but learning to recognize them quickly and respond thoughtfully rather than reactively. Common leadership triggers include:

Being Questioned or Challenged: Some leaders interpret questions about their decisions as personal attacks on their competence, leading to defensive responses that shut down dialogue.

Lack of Urgency: Leaders who value speed and action often become frustrated with team members who want to slow down and think through implications.

Perceived Incompetence: Watching someone struggle with something you could do easily can trigger impatience and the urge to take over rather than coach.

Feeling Unheard: When you feel like your ideas aren't being considered or implemented, it can trigger reactions about respect and influence.

Loss of Control: Situations where you can't directly influence outcomes can trigger anxiety and micromanagement behaviors.

When you notice a strong emotional reaction starting, use this four-step S.T.O.P. process for managing those triggers.

(S)top: Pause before you speak or act. Take a breath. Create space between the trigger and your response.

(T)hink: Ask yourself, "What's really happening here? What am I making this mean? Is my reaction proportional to the situation?"

(O)ptions: Consider multiple ways to respond. What would serve the situation best? What response aligns with your values and leadership goals?

(P)roceed: Choose your response deliberately rather than reacting automatically. You can always ask for time to think if you need it.

This isn't about suppressing emotions or pretending you don't have reactions. It's about creating enough space to choose your response based on your values and goals rather than your immediate emotional impulse.

Building Your Reflection Practice

Self-awareness isn't a destination—it's an ongoing practice. The most effective leaders I work with have developed consistent habits for reflection and self-examination. They regularly step back from the action to examine their effectiveness, impact, and growth.

However, the key to sustainable reflection practice is finding a rhythm that works long-term without becoming burdensome. I recommend committing to these practices for 90 days initially, then adjusting based on what you learn about yourself and what proves most valuable.

Daily Reflection Questions (90-Day Commitment):
- End each day by asking yourself these three questions:
- What did I do well as a leader today?
- What would I do differently if I could replay one interaction?
- What did I learn about myself today?

After 90 days, you may find that 2-3 times per week works better for your schedule while still maintaining the benefit.

Weekly Leadership Review (Ongoing):
Set aside 20 minutes each week to reflect on:
- Which of my core values did I honor most this week? Which did I compromise?
- What feedback did I receive (directly or indirectly) about my leadership?

- Where did I operate from my strengths? Where did my development areas create challenges?
- What patterns am I noticing in my leadership approach?

Monthly 360-Degree Check-ins (Quarterly After First Year):

Initially, have informal conversations monthly with people who see your leadership from different angles—your supervisor, peers, direct reports, and even internal customers. After the first year, quarterly check-ins often provide sufficient input without creating feedback fatigue. Ask:

- What's one thing I should keep doing as a leader?
- What's one thing I should start doing?
- What's one thing I should stop doing?

The Feedback Loop: Seeking Input Without Defensiveness

One of the biggest barriers to self-awareness is our natural tendency to defend our current self-image. We filter feedback through our existing beliefs about ourselves, often dismissing input that doesn't match our self-perception.

Presence-driven leaders approach feedback differently. They see it as data, not judgment. They understand that other people's perceptions are their reality, even if those perceptions don't match the leader's intentions.

Creating Safe Feedback Conversations:

Ask specific questions: Instead of "How am I doing?" ask "What's one thing I could do to be more effective in our team meetings?" Specific questions generate more useful responses.

Listen without explaining: When someone gives you feedback, resist the urge to justify your actions or explain your intentions. Just listen and ask clarifying questions.

Thank people for their honesty: Feedback takes courage. Acknowledge that and express genuine appreciation, especially for difficult feedback.

Follow up: Let people know how you've acted on their input. This encourages future feedback and shows you take their perspectives seriously.

Model vulnerability: Share your own development goals and ask for help. When leaders are open about their growth areas, it creates a sense of permission for others to be honest about their observations.

Self-awareness without action is just interesting information. The goal is to translate your insights into specific development activities that will enhance your leadership presence. Your development plan should address three areas:

Leverage Your Strengths: How will you create more opportunities to use your natural leadership abilities? How can you build on what you already do well?

Address Development Areas: What specific skills or behaviors do you need to develop? What support do you need to make meaningful progress?

Live Your Values: How will you ensure your daily actions reflect your core values, especially in challenging situations?

For each development area, create SMART goals (specific, measurable, achievable, relevant, time-bound) with specific timelines, success metrics, and accountability measures. Share these goals with a trusted colleague or mentor who can provide ongoing feedback and support.

Self-awareness isn't a box you check once and move on. It's a lifelong practice that deepens with experience and reflection. The leaders with the greatest presence are those who remain curious about themselves, are open to feedback, and are committed to continuous growth.

As you develop greater self-awareness, you'll notice several shifts in your leadership, including increased authenticity. You'll feel more comfortable leading from your genuine self rather than performing a role. You will see better decision-making as clear values and an honest self-assessment will guide you toward choices that align with your principles and capabilities. Stronger relationships because when you understand your impact on others, you can adjust your approach to communicate more effectively and build better connections. Greater resilience as self-aware leaders bounce back from setbacks more quickly because they can learn from experience without taking everything personally. And enhanced credibility as people trust leaders who know themselves and are honest about their strengths and limitations.

The inner work of leadership is challenging because it requires confronting uncomfortable truths about yourself. But it's also liberating because it frees you from the exhausting work of maintaining a false image.

When you lead from genuine self-knowledge, you can focus your energy on serving others and achieving results rather than protecting your ego or proving your worth. That's when leadership becomes less about what you do and more about who you are.

CHAPTER 3

Coaching Through Challenges

The call came on a Tuesday morning. One of my team members had made a significant error that affected a high-profile client event. My first instinct was to fix it myself—I knew exactly what needed to be done, and speed was critical. But as I reached for the phone to start making calls, I stopped.

This was a choice moment. I could solve the problem quickly and move on, or I could use this challenge as an opportunity to develop my team member's problem-solving capabilities. The first approach would get immediate results. The second would build long-term capacity.

I chose to coach. That decision led to one of the most powerful leadership conversations I've ever had. Instead of swooping in to save the day, I helped my team member think through the situation, identify solutions, and take ownership of the resolution. The client's issue was resolved successfully, and more importantly, that team member never made a similar mistake again. In fact, she became one of my strongest problem-solvers.

This is the first pillar of presence-driven leadership: the ability to coach through challenges rather than manage problems. It's the difference between building people and just getting things done. It's about actively developing people with empathy and feedback, creating an environment where praise, feedback, and accountability aren't just tools—they're relationship builders.

The Coaching Mindset Shift

Most leaders approach problems with a fix-it mentality. When something goes wrong, they jump into solution mode. When someone struggles, they provide answers. When performance needs improvement, they give direction. This "fix-it" approach feels efficient in the moment, but it creates several long-term problems:

Dependency: Team members learn to bring you problems instead of solutions because they know you'll figure it out for them.

Limited Growth: People don't develop their own problem-solving capabilities when you consistently solve things for them.

Bottlenecks: Everything runs through you, limiting your team's capacity to operate independently.

Disengagement: Team members feel less ownership and investment when they're not involved in creating solutions.

Coaching-oriented leaders approach challenges differently. Instead of providing answers, they ask questions that help people discover solutions. Instead of taking over when someone struggles, they provide support while maintaining accountability. Instead of micromanaging performance, they create environments where people can succeed.

This shift requires what I call "productive patience"—the discipline to slow down in the moment so you can speed up in the long run. It means resisting the urge to jump in and fix everything yourself, even when you know you could do it faster.

Research by the International Coach Federation shows that organizations with strong coaching cultures report significantly higher employee engagement and revenue growth compared to their peers. Additionally, 70% of coached individuals report improved work performance (ICF/HCI, *Building a Coaching Culture*, ICF Global Coaching Study).

But here's what the research doesn't capture: the profound satisfaction that comes from watching someone you've coached succeed independently. There's no comparison between the temporary gratification of solving a problem yourself and the lasting impact of helping someone else develop the capability to solve it.

One of the most significant mindset shifts for presence-driven leaders is moving from punishment-based discipline to development-focused coaching. When someone makes a mistake or falls short of expectations, your first question should be: "How can I help this person grow from this experience?"

This doesn't mean lowering standards or avoiding difficult conversations. It means approaching performance issues as coaching opportunities rather than disciplinary actions.

When you have a team member who keeps making the same mistakes or doesn't understand their tasks, you must have a private conversation. This offers personalized coaching and counseling, making life easier for everyone.

As a leader, when you coach folks (even if they are failing), you keep coaching them all the way up to the end. You may be able to turn your team member around and intervene. This humanizing approach contrasts with the idea of disciplining someone—discipline implies you have already given up on them.

Traditional Discipline Approach:
- Focus on what went wrong
- Emphasize consequences
- Position leader as judge
- Create defensive responses
- Results in compliance without understanding

Development-Focused Coaching:
- Focus on learning and improvement
- Emphasize future success
- Position leader as partner
- Create collaborative problem-solving
- Results in ownership and capability building

Consider the difference between these two conversations about a missed deadline:

Traditional Approach: "This project was due yesterday, and you're just getting it to me now. This is unacceptable, and it can't happen again. I need you to be more organized and manage your time better."

Coaching Approach: "I noticed the project came in a day later than we agreed. Help me understand what happened and what we can learn from this to prevent similar situations from happening in the future."

The first conversation focuses on blame and generates defensiveness. The second creates an opportunity for problem-solving and skill development.

The GROW Model for Coaching Conversations

The most effective coaching conversations follow a structured approach that helps people systematically think through challenges. The GROW model provides a framework that any leader can use:

(G)oal: What are we trying to achieve?

(R)eality: What's the current situation?

(O)ptions: What possibilities exist?

(W)ay Forward: What specific actions will we take?

Let me show you how this works with a real scenario from my experience.

The Situation: A front desk supervisor was struggling with staff scheduling conflicts that were affecting guest service. Team members frequently called in sick, and the remaining staff felt overwhelmed and frustrated. Here's how I coached her through the challenge.

Goal Phase:

"What would success look like for you in this situation?"

"Ideally, I'd have consistent staffing so guests don't experience delays, and my team would feel supported rather than constantly stressed."

Reality Phase:

"What's happening now that's different from that ideal?"

"We're short-staffed at least three days a week. People are calling in sick more often, and when they do, the remaining team has to handle twice the workload. I think some of the sick calls aren't legitimate—people are just burned out."

Options Phase:

"What are some different ways you could approach this?"

"Well, I could schedule the person less days until their attendance improves, but that feels punitive. I could cross-train more people so we have backup coverage. I could also look at whether we have the right number of people scheduled in the first place—maybe we're understaffing to begin with."

Way Forward Phase:

"Which of those options feels most promising to start with?"

"I think I should first analyze our scheduling patterns to see if we're setting ourselves up for failure. Then I'd like to cross-train three more people so we have better coverage. And I want to have one-on-one conversations with the team to understand what's driving the stress."

Notice that I didn't provide the solution. I asked questions that helped her think through the problem systematically and arrive at her own action plan. This approach takes longer in the moment, but it will build problem-solving capacity that will serve her in future challenges.

The Foundation of Empathy-Led Leadership:

Try to understand what the root issue is, instead of acting punitively. Empathy comes into play in so many different ways when you're coaching through challenges.

Does your team have the right tools, supplies, training, and motivation to get their job done? Be sure to take those things into consideration. There are outside circumstances that could be influencing their work, including personal and family matters. This doesn't mean team members get a pass every time something personal happens, but empathy-led leadership will go a lot further in figuring out a path forward.

Questions to Ask Before Assuming Performance Issues:
- Do they have the necessary resources and tools?
- Have they received adequate training for this responsibility?
- Are there personal circumstances affecting their performance?
- Is the expectation clearly understood?
- Are there systemic barriers preventing success?

Sometimes what looks like a performance problem is actually a support problem. Before you coach someone on their approach, make sure they have what they need to succeed.

The Power of Real-Time Coaching and Recognition

In every leadership role I've held, I have never worked at a location where anyone, myself included, returned home and told their significant other, "My boss/company has given me way too much praise!"

As a rule, I make a point to thank my team. I go out of my way to publicly thank them during project visits or property walkthroughs. I always thank them for their hard work and hospitality, but I also quickly point out any shortfalls I see.

Think of it like a football game, where coaches talk to team members on the sidelines, offering advice on how to improve their game. Watch when a player makes a mistake or gets close to making an error—you'll see a coach advising players: "move to the left, move to the right, back up, fall back, slow down, speed up." You also hear, "Great job! Nice job! Do it again, do it like that all the time, way to go!"

Leaders are like coaches—affirming and advising team players. That's how I see it. As a leader, I commit to constantly giving my team feedback, coaching, and praise. I offer this coaching and praise in the workplace and on the fly.

Minor issues should be addressed immediately and directly. If I see someone struggling with a process or making a small error, I'll name what I see right away: "I noticed you're having trouble with that system—let me show you a quicker way." When significant issues arise, pull the person aside for a private conversation. A presence-driven leader wouldn't dare embarrass a team member in front of others. We handle bigger challenges with dignity and privacy. This real-time approach prevents small issues from becoming big problems and shows your team that you're invested in their success, not just waiting to catch them doing something wrong.

Effective coaching requires psychological safety—the belief that you can speak up, ask questions, make mistakes, and be vulnerable without fear of negative consequences. Google's Project Aristotle research found that psychological safety was the most important factor in team effectiveness, more predictive of success than individual talent or team composition. Without psychological safety, people won't bring you their real challenges, and coaching conversations become surface-level rather than transformative.

How to Build Psychological Safety

Model vulnerability: Share your own mistakes and learning experiences. When leaders are open about their imperfections, it gives others permission to be honest about theirs.

Respond to failure with curiosity, not judgment: When someone makes a mistake, your first response should be questions, not criticism. "What happened here? What can we learn? How can we prevent this in the future?"

Make feedback a gift: Help your team understand that feedback is a gift. If someone wants to get better at what they're doing on their own, they may be able to do it alone, but it will probably take much longer. Chances are, if they have someone coaching them and giving them feedback, they'll figure out their task quicker and more efficiently.

Remove punitive language: I intentionally remove the term "disciplinary" from my organizations. This framing places your teams in a teacher-student or parent-child dynamic. We are all on the same team. I intentionally cultivate an equal learning and growth mindset and culture.

Ask "What would help?" rather than "What went wrong?" This shifts the conversation from blame to support and solutions.

Celebrate learning from mistakes: When someone brings you a problem they created, thank them for their honesty before you address the issue. This encourages transparency.

Be consistent in your responses: If you're supportive and curious when things go well, but critical and impatient when they don't, people will learn to hide problems from you.

Advanced Coaching Techniques

Once you've mastered the basics of coaching conversations, these advanced techniques will help you have an even greater impact:

The Scaling Question: On a scale of 1-10, how confident are you that you can handle this situation? What would it take to move that number up by just one point?

This helps people identify specific, manageable steps toward improvement rather than feeling overwhelmed by the full challenge.

The Best Self Question: Think about a time when you handled a similar situation really well. What did you do differently that might apply here?

This connects people to their own past successes and builds confidence that they have the capability to succeed.

The Stakeholder Perspective: If [key stakeholder] were sitting here with us, what would they want us to focus on?

This helps broaden perspective beyond immediate concerns to consider broader impact and priorities.

The Future Success Question: Imagine it's six months from now and this challenge has been completely resolved. Looking back, what were the key things that made the difference?

This creates a vision of success and works backward to identify critical actions.

Individual coaching conversations are powerful, but creating a team culture where everyone coaches each other multiplies that impact exponentially.

Model Coaching Language: Use coaching questions in team meetings. Instead of providing all the answers yourself, ask, "What options do we have here?" or "What do you think would work best?"

Teach the GROW Model: Share the framework with your team so they can use it with each other and in their own problem-solving.

Create Peer Coaching Partnerships: Pair team members to support each other's development goals. This spreads coaching beyond just manager-to-employee relationships.

Celebrate Coaching Moments: When you see team members helping each other grow and learn, acknowledge it publicly. "I loved seeing how you helped Sarah think through that challenge rather than just giving her the answer."

Make Time for Reflection: Build regular time into team meetings for people to share what they're learning and how they're growing.

Coaching Through Different Types of Challenges

Not every challenge requires the same coaching approach. Here's how to adapt your style based on the situation:

Skill-Based Challenges: When someone lacks the technical knowledge or ability to do something, coaching focuses on learning and development.
- "What resources would help you build this capability?"
- "Who could you observe or learn from?"
- "What's the first step in developing this skill?"

Confidence-Based Challenges: When someone has the ability but lacks confidence, coaching focuses on building belief and reducing anxiety.
- "What evidence do you have that you can handle this?"
- "What's the worst that could realistically happen?"
- "What support do you need to feel more confident?"

Motivation-Based Challenges: When someone has lost enthusiasm or engagement, coaching focuses on reconnecting to purpose and meaning.
- "What originally excited you about this work?"
- "How does this connect to your broader goals?"
- "What would make this more meaningful for you?"

System-Based Challenges: When the problem is organizational rather than individual, coaching focuses on navigating and influencing systems.
- "What parts of this system can you influence?"
- "Who else needs to be involved to create change?"
- "What small experiments could we try?"

The Long-Term Impact of Coaching Leadership

When you consistently coach through challenges rather than simply solving problems, several things happen over time:

Increased autonomy: Your team members become more independent and require less supervision because they've developed their own problem-solving capabilities.

Better decision-making: People who have been coached through challenges learn to think more systematically and consider broader implications when making decisions.

Higher engagement: Team members feel more ownership and investment in their work when they've been involved in creating solutions rather than just implementing directives.

Stronger relationships: The coaching process builds trust and rapport between you and your team members as they experience your investment in their growth.

Organizational resilience: Teams that have been coached through challenges are better equipped to handle future obstacles independently.

While coaching is a powerful tool, it's important to recognize when more direct intervention is needed. Coaching works best when people have the basic willingness and capability to improve. If you've coached someone consistently and there's no progress, you may need to provide more direct training or support. Sometimes people need explicit instruction before they can benefit from coaching. Also, address systemic barriers if organizational policies or resources are preventing success because coaching alone won't solve the problem. In rare cases, someone may not be in the right role for their skills and interests, and continuing to coach isn't serving anyone well.

The key is to coach consistently and document your efforts so that if you do need to take other actions, you can do so knowing you've given the person every opportunity to succeed. Remember that coaching isn't just about solving immediate problems or developing specific skills. It's about building relationships and demonstrating that you value people's growth and potential. Every coaching conversation sends a message: "I believe you're capable of more than you're currently doing, and I'm willing to invest my time in helping you get there." That message transforms how people experience your leadership and how they show up for the work. It's the foundation of the trust and influence that allow presence-driven leaders to achieve extraordinary results through ordinary people. When you coach through challenges, you're not just solving today's problems—you're building tomorrow's leaders. And that's how presence-driven leadership creates lasting impact that extends far beyond any individual role or organization.

CHAPTER 4

Influence Without Authority

As a front desk agent, I learned that influence doesn't come from title—it comes from trust. You are the hotel hub. When something goes wrong with the A/C in the room, the guest doesn't call engineering; they call the front desk. When there is a problem with the cleanliness of their room, they don't call housekeeping; they call the front desk. This is true for several other scenarios.

If you're going to survive getting your face ripped off by guests and being successful at the desk, you learn to think quickly on your feet. You become an expert problem solver. To solve problems, you get really good at building relationships with your contacts in each department. When you're in a hard spot with a guest, you can get the help you need and get it quickly.

This early lesson became the foundation of everything I learned about influence without authority. The front desk agent has no formal power over engineering, housekeeping, or any other department, yet success depends entirely on your ability to get those departments to prioritize your requests and respond quickly to guest needs.

That's the essence of influence without authority—the ability to drive outcomes and create change without relying on your position to make things happen. It's the second pillar of presence-driven leadership: influencing up, down, and across to drive outcomes without relying on authority.

Here's the truth about leadership in today's organizations: Most of the time, you need to influence people you don't control. The flat organizational structures, matrix reporting relationships, and cross-functional teams that define modern work mean that getting things done requires influence across levels and departments.

Even when you do have formal authority over people, relying on that authority is often counterproductive. Position-based compliance gets you minimal effort and temporary results. Influence-based commitment gets you discretionary effort and sustainable change.

Research by the Center for Creative Leadership found that the ability to influence without authority is a key predictor of executive success, as executives spend significant time working with people over whom they have no direct authority. Yet most leadership development focuses on managing direct reports rather than building influence with peers, superiors, and stakeholders across the organization.

I learned this ability as a front desk agent working with all of the departments in the hotel and working on group assignments in college which was a perfect set up for my first management position when I graduated. I became a conference services manager, essentially the general manager for assigned groups who had several touch points to almost every department in the resort. In this role, I had to convey many details clearly and solve problems. I coordinated a lot of moving parts to pull off a flawless group stay.

The conference services manager role perfectly illustrates influence without authority. You're responsible for the guest experience, but you don't manage housekeeping, food and beverage, engineering, or any of the departments that directly impact that experience. Your success depends entirely on your ability to influence others to prioritize your groups and execute flawlessly.

From my first department head role as director of front office, I made it a point to build relationships with my other counterparts in my market. I wanted to know what the best theme parties were, best vendors to use, and latest food and beverage trends as a convention services manager. As the director of front office, I wanted to know whether we were getting the best rates, what the most frequent customer demands were, how my competitors were responding, and how we could do it better.

I have carried this mindset into every role I have held since then. When I moved into a new market, it became more urgent for me to make sure I understood what was going on, not just in my hotels, but in the larger market. Now, for example, I still research trends, whether it's searching for the top talent or wage and benefits benchmarks.

This approach taught me that influence is built through relationships, and relationships are built through genuine interest in others' success and challenges. When you understand what your counterparts are dealing with, what they're measured on, and what would make their jobs easier, you can frame your requests in ways that align with their interests.

The Three Pillars of Influence

Effective influence without authority rests on three foundational elements: credibility, connection, and compelling communication. Master these three areas, and you'll be able to drive results regardless of your position on the organizational chart.

Pillar 1: Credibility

Credibility is your influence bank account. Every interaction either makes a deposit (building trust and respect) or makes a withdrawal (diminishing your influence). The leaders who can influence without authority have built substantial account balances through consistent, competent, and trustworthy behavior.

In the hospitality industry, credibility is everything. If the engineering team doesn't trust that your "emergency" is actually urgent, they won't prioritize your request. If housekeeping believes you throw them under the bus when guests complain, they'll be less responsive when you need quick room turnarounds.

There are two primary ways to build credibility: competence and character.

Building Credibility Through Competence

Deliver on your commitments: When you tell engineering you need a room fixed by 3 PM, make sure there's actually a guest checking in at 3 PM. Don't cry wolf.

Bring value to every interaction: When you call housekeeping about a room issue, also let them know about compliments guests have shared about their work.

Know your stuff: Stay current with industry trends, competitor actions, and market conditions. Be the person others come to for insights.

Admit what you don't know: If a guest asks about local attractions and you're not sure, say so, and find someone who can help rather than guessing.

Building Credibility Through Character

Keep confidences: When a department head shares sensitive information with you, protect it. Nothing destroys influence faster than being seen as untrustworthy with information.

Give credit generously: When a group event goes perfectly, make sure the departments that made it happen get recognized publicly.

Follow through on small things: If you promise to send meeting notes by the end of the day, do it. Credibility is built in the details.

Be consistent across relationships: Your character should be the same whether you're talking to the most senior leader or the coordinator.

Pillar 2: Connection

Influence isn't about manipulation—it's about alignment. The most effective influencers understand what motivates the people they need to work with and find ways to connect their requests to those motivations.

For any significant influence opportunity, understand your key stakeholders:

Decision-makers: Who has the final say?
Influencers: Who do the decision-makers listen to?
Implementers: Who will actually do the work?
Potential resisters: Who might oppose the change and why?

For each stakeholder, understand:
- Their current priorities and pressures
- What success looks like from their perspective
- What they're measured on or rewarded for
- Their preferred communication style
- Their past experiences with similar initiatives

Building Connection Through Curiosity

The fastest way to build a connection is to be genuinely curious about others' perspectives and challenges. In my roles, I made it a point to understand:

- What challenges were my counterparts in other departments facing?
- What were their biggest frustrations with current processes?
- What would make their jobs easier or more successful?
- How could I help them look good to their supervisors?

The WIIFM Principle (What's in It for Me)

Every person you're trying to influence is unconsciously asking, "What's in it for me?" Your job is to answer that question clearly and compellingly. In hospitality, this might be:

- How will this improve guest satisfaction scores that affect bonuses?
- How will this reduce the number of complaints they have to handle?
- How will this make their daily work more efficient?
- How will this help them avoid overtime or weekend work?
- How will this make them look good to senior leadership?

Pillar 3: Compelling Communication

Different people are persuaded by different types of communication. The most influential leaders use three primary approaches strategically:

Data-Driven Influence

Some people need to see the numbers before they'll commit to change. For analytical personalities, lead with:

Clear metrics: "Guest satisfaction scores increased 12% after implementing this process at our sister property."

Cost-benefit analysis: "This will cost us $5,000 upfront but save $30,000 annually in labor costs."

Risk assessment: "If we don't address this, we're looking at potential safety violations that could result in significant fines."

Benchmarking: "Our competitors are already doing this—we're risking market share by not keeping up."

Story-Driven Influence

Others are moved by narrative and real experiences. For relationship-focused personalities, share:

Guest impact stories: "I had a guest yesterday whose entire conference was saved because engineering responded so quickly to the A/C issue."

Team success stories: "When the Denver property implemented this, their employee satisfaction scores went up 20%."

Personal experiences: "When I was managing conferences, this type of coordination made the difference between disaster and success."

Vision narratives: "Imagine if our guests consistently rated us as the best service in the market because every department worked this seamlessly together."

Relationship-Driven Influence

Some people are most influenced by who else is involved or supporting an initiative:

Leadership support: "The GM is fully behind this approach and sees it as critical to our success."

Peer influence: "The other department heads are excited about this because it will reduce conflicts between our teams."

Industry validation: "The consultant who helped Company X achieve similar results recommends this strategy."

Coalition building: "I've talked to leaders in sales, operations, and finance, and everyone agrees this is the right direction."

Influence Strategies for Different Organizational Levels

Your influence approach should adapt based on whether you're trying to influence up, across, or down in the organization.

Influencing Up: Leading Your Leader

Influencing senior leaders requires understanding that they are typically:

- Time-constrained and want bottom-line impact
- Focused on strategic rather than tactical issues
- Concerned with risk and organizational implications
- Influenced by data and business cases

Strategies for Upward Influence:

Frame issues in business terms: Don't just present operational problems—present business impact. "This isn't just a staffing issue—it's affecting our ability to meet guest satisfaction targets."

Come with solutions, not just problems: Leaders want to know what you recommend, not just what's wrong.

Understand their priorities: What are they being measured on? What keeps them up at night? How does your request connect to their success?

Respect their time: Be concise, well-prepared, and clear about what you need from them.

Make them look good: How can supporting your initiative enhance their reputation or help them achieve their goals?

Influencing Across: Building Peer Alliances

Influencing peers can be the most challenging because you're equals with competing priorities and limited time. Peer influence requires:

Reciprocity: What can you offer in return? How can you help them achieve their goals?

Shared interests: Where do your objectives align? Focus on common ground rather than competing priorities.

Mutual respect: Acknowledge their expertise and constraints. Don't approach peer influence as if you know better.

Collaboration: Frame requests as joint problem-solving rather than asking for favors.

Long-term thinking: Build relationships before you need them. Invest in peer relationships when you don't need anything.

Influencing Down: Leading Without Micromanaging

Even with direct reports, influence is often more effective than authority. People who feel influenced rather than commanded:
- Take more ownership of outcomes
- Show greater creativity in problem-solving
- Require less supervision
- Stay more engaged during challenges

Help people understand how their role contributes to company values and business objectives. Connect their work to the larger purpose. The largest part of the workforce today is millennials and Gen Z combined, and it is absolutely crucial to make this connection. These generations want to understand not just what they're doing, but why it matters and how it fits into the bigger picture. Involve them in decision-making because people support what they help create. Provide autonomy with accountability by giving people freedom in how they achieve clear objectives. Recognize and celebrate their successes as acknowledgment is one of the most powerful influence tools. Use your authority to eliminate obstacles that prevent their success.

The Art of Strategic Networking

I live by this quote: "Network. Network. Network—and when you think you are done networking? Network some more."

Networking often gets a bad reputation because people approach it wrong. They see it as using people to get ahead rather than building mutually beneficial relationships. Presence-driven leaders understand that networking is actually about creating value for others while building a matrix of relationships that can help you solve problems and create opportunities.

Reframe Networking as Relationship Building

Instead of "What can this person do for me?" ask "How can I be helpful to this person?" When you lead with generosity, people remember and reciprocate. This might mean:

- Sharing vendor recommendations with counterparts at other properties
- Providing industry intelligence about emerging trends and best practices
- Introducing contacts who could help solve each other's challenges
- Sharing innovative approaches that have worked well for your team

The 70-20-10 Rule

70% of your networking time should be spent with people at your level, building peer relationships and sharing knowledge

20% with people above you in the organization, learning from their experience and understanding their perspectives

10% with people below you in the organization, developing them and building future leadership

Networking Activities That Build Influence

Industry involvement: Participate in professional associations, conferences, and local business groups where you can meet people outside your organization.

Cross-functional project work: Volunteer for initiatives that put you in contact with people from other departments.

Internal mentoring: Offer to mentor high-potential employees from other departments.

Knowledge sharing: Host training sessions, share industry articles, or present best practices at company meetings.

Market intelligence: Be the person who knows what's happening in your market and share that knowledge generously.

Overcoming Resistance and Objections

Not everyone will be immediately receptive to your influence attempts. The key is understanding why people resist and addressing those underlying concerns.

Resource concerns: They're worried about time, money, or energy required.

Fear of change: People worry about how changes will affect their daily routines.

Past experiences: Previous initiatives failed or created more work without benefits.

Competing priorities: They have other urgent demands on their attention.

Lack of trust: They don't believe the change will actually help them.

The Feel-Felt-Found Technique

When someone expresses resistance, use this three-step approach:

Feel: "I understand how you feel about this. It does require learning new processes."

Felt: "Other department heads felt the same way when we first discussed this approach."

Found: "What they found, though, is that it actually reduced their workload once everyone got used to the new system."

This technique acknowledges their resistance without dismissing it, connects them to others who have successfully navigated similar concerns, and opens the door for further discussion.

Building Coalitions for Change

Some initiatives are too big for individual influence. They require coalition building—bringing together multiple stakeholders who can collectively drive change.

Identify champions: Who already supports this change and could advocate for it?

Find fence-sitters: Who could be convinced with the right approach?

Understand opposition: Who will resist and why? Can their concerns be addressed?

Create early wins: Start with small successes that build momentum for larger changes.

Communicate progress: Keep coalition members informed about successes and next steps.

Successful coalitions often start with departments that share common challenges. If you're trying to introduce a new initiative, look to the departments that have a shared interest in the success of this initiative.

The Long-Term Impact of Influence Without Authority

When you consistently influence without relying on authority, several things happen:

Enhanced reputation: People see you as someone who gets things done and can work effectively across the organization.

Increased access: Leaders and colleagues seek your input on decisions because they trust your judgment and approach.

Greater impact: You can drive change and achieve results far beyond what your formal role would suggest.

Expanded opportunities: People think of you for new roles and projects because of your proven ability to work with diverse stakeholders.

Stronger relationships: The collaborative approach to influence builds lasting connections throughout the organization.

This is exactly what happened throughout my career in hospitality. The relationships I built as a front desk agent served me as a conference services manager. The network I developed as a department head opened doors when I moved into regional and corporate roles. Each role built on the influence foundation established in previous positions.

While influence without authority is a powerful tool, there are times when it's not sufficient:

Emergency situations: When guest safety is at risk, immediate action may be required regardless of preferences.

Legal or compliance issues: Some requirements aren't negotiable and must be mandated.

Repeated non-compliance: When someone consistently ignores influence attempts, formal authority may be the only option.

Resource allocation: Final decisions about budgets and staffing often require positional authority.

The key is using authority as a last resort, not a first response. When you do need to use formal power, you can do so more effectively because people know you've tried other approaches first.

Remember that influence without authority isn't just a technique—it's a leadership philosophy. It's based on the belief that people do their best work when they're committed to outcomes rather than simply compliant with directives.

When you master influence without authority, you create a foundation of trust and credibility that amplifies every other aspect of your leadership. People listen when you speak because they know you've earned the right to be heard. They follow your lead because they believe in your judgment and trust your intentions.

This sets the stage for the third pillar of presence-driven leadership: leading with conviction. When you have the trust that comes from effective coaching and the credibility that comes from skillful influence, you can make the hard decisions and take the principled stands that define truly transformational leadership.

CHAPTER 5

Leading With Conviction

I certainly don't claim to be a choir boy. Heck, I haven't been to church in years, nor do I claim to be a perfect person. Having said that, I believe that you must have a steady moral and ethical compass in order to stand on business.

Conviction in leadership isn't about being perfect or having all the answers. It's about knowing what you stand for and being willing to act on those principles, even when it's difficult. But here's what many leaders get wrong: they think conviction means being rigid, inflexible, or unwilling to consider other perspectives.

True conviction is different. Conviction means you stand for something, but you are also coachable, agile, and people-focused. It's the third pillar of presence-driven leadership: leading from your values as your compass while remaining open to new information and different approaches.

This chapter is about finding that balance—how to lead with strong convictions while maintaining the humility and adaptability that makes you an effective leader.

The Foundation of Conviction: Your Moral and Ethical Compass

You must check your sources, collaborate with a variety of different perspectives, be aware of current events that can shift what's happening on the ground, and understand if that is all in alignment. Do this, and your team will follow you.

A steady moral and ethical compass don't mean you have to be perfect. It means you have clear principles that guide your decisions, especially when you're under pressure or facing difficult choices. These principles serve as a foundation people can count on, regardless of changing circumstances.

Building Your Ethical Foundation:

Identify your non-negotiables: What principles will you never compromise, no matter the pressure or potential benefit? These might include honesty, respect for people, safety, or fairness.

Understand your "why": What deeper purpose drives your leadership? What impact do you want to have on the people you lead and the organization you serve?

Check your sources: Make sure your decisions are based on accurate information from credible sources. Don't make conviction-based decisions on incomplete or biased data.

Seek diverse perspectives: Conviction doesn't mean isolation. Actively seek input from people with different backgrounds, experiences, and viewpoints before making important decisions.

Stay current: Be aware of current events, industry trends, and cultural shifts that might affect your team and organization. Context matters when you're making principle-based decisions.

The leaders I respect most aren't those who never make mistakes—they're the ones who make decisions based on clear principles and own the outcomes, whether positive or negative.

The Power of Principled Decision-Making

When you lead with conviction, you're not just making decisions based on immediate circumstances or political convenience. You're making choices that align with your values and serve the long-term good of your team and organization.

The Conviction Decision-Making Process:
1. **Clarify the situation:** What decision needs to be made? What are the stakes and who will be affected?
2. **Identify your relevant principles:** Which of your core values apply to this situation? What would acting on these values look like?
3. **Gather information:** What facts do you need? Whose perspectives should you consider? What are the potential consequences of different choices?
4. **Consider options:** What alternatives exist? How does each option align with your principles? What are the trade-offs?
5. **Decide and act:** Choose the option that best serves your principles and the greater good, even if it's not the easiest or most popular choice.
6. **Own the outcome:** Take responsibility for the results, learn from what happens, and adjust your approach for future decisions.

This process helps ensure that your decisions are both principled and practical. You're not making choices in isolation—you're considering input, consequences, and context while staying true to your core values.

Balancing Conviction with Humility

Get familiar with having humility. There may be times when your boss simply says no. I am the first to admit that it pains me when I hear that word, and I see it as a challenge. Yet I have seen leaders self-destruct because of their inability to let something go.

One of the biggest challenges for conviction-driven leaders is learning when to stand firm and when to be flexible. The key is understanding the difference between your core principles (which shouldn't be compromised) and your preferred methods (which should be adaptable).

Core principles are your fundamental values—things like integrity, respect for people, or commitment to quality. These should remain constant regardless of circumstances. Preferred methods are your approaches, strategies, and tactics for achieving goals. These should be flexible based on feedback, changing conditions, and new information.

If I see a way that does work but run into a different suggestion from the team, I will course correct and let them take the win. Or if my boss is saying no, and I have a handle on my relationships, industry trends, and local market data, I can usually parlay another way to get something accomplished. I can turn a "no" into a "what if we do this?" and I can get a "yes."

This is the essence of conviction with humility—staying committed to your principles while remaining flexible about how you achieve them.

When to Stand Firm:
- Core values are at stake
- Ethical principles are being compromised
- Safety or legal requirements are involved

- The long-term integrity of the team or organization is threatened

When to Be Flexible:
- The principle can be achieved through different methods
- New information suggests a better approach
- Team input reveals blind spots in your thinking
- Changing circumstances require adaptation

The key is understanding the difference between principled persistence and stubborn inflexibility. Principled persistence means continuing to advocate for what you believe is right while remaining open to different approaches and timing.

Strategies for Principled Persistence:

Reframe the conversation: Instead of accepting "no" as final, try "Help me understand your concerns" or "What would need to be different for this to work?"

Provide additional context: Sometimes resistance comes from incomplete information. Share data, trends, or perspectives that might change the equation.

Propose alternatives: If your initial approach isn't acceptable, offer different methods for achieving the same principle-based outcome.

Address underlying concerns: Get to the root of why someone is saying no. Often, addressing the underlying worry opens up new possibilities.

Choose your timing: Sometimes the right idea at the wrong time gets rejected. Be willing to wait for better circumstances while keeping the principle alive.

Build coalitions: Find others who share your conviction and can help advocate for the principle from different perspectives.

The key is persistence without personal attachment to a specific outcome. You're advocating for principles, not defending your ego.

Courageous Leadership in Difficult Moments

Leading with conviction sometimes requires courage (the willingness to do what's right even when it's difficult, unpopular, or risky). These moments define your leadership and determine whether people will trust you when the stakes are high.

Types of Leadership Courage:

Moral Courage: Standing up for what's right when others are compromising or looking the other way.

Social Courage: Speaking truth to power or challenging popular but misguided decisions.

Physical Courage: Taking action when there are real risks to safety, career, or well-being.

Emotional Courage: Having difficult conversations, addressing performance issues, or delivering bad news with honesty and compassion.

Intellectual Courage: Admitting mistakes, changing positions when presented with new evidence, or challenging conventional wisdom.

Building Your Courage Capacity:

Start small: Practice standing up for principles in low-stakes situations to build your courage muscle for bigger moments.

Know your values: The clearer you are about what you stand for, the easier it becomes to act courageously when those values are tested.

Build support networks: Surround yourself with people who share your values and will support you when you need to take difficult stands.

Focus on service: Courage becomes easier when you're focused on serving others rather than protecting yourself.

Prepare for consequences: Understand the potential risks of courageous action and decide in advance that the principle is worth the cost.

Leading Change with Conviction

Conviction-driven leaders often find themselves leading change efforts because they see gaps between current reality and their vision of what should be. Leading change requires conviction because there will always be resistance, setbacks, and pressure to give up.

The Change Leadership Process:

Build the case for change: Help people understand why the current state is unsustainable and how change aligns with shared values.

Create a compelling vision: Paint a picture of what success looks like that connects to people's deeper motivations.

Address resistance with empathy: Understand that resistance often comes from fear or past negative experiences with change.

Start with willing participants: Build momentum by working with people who are ready to embrace change before trying to convince the skeptics.

Celebrate small wins: Recognize progress along the way to maintain momentum and show that the change is working.

Stay committed through setbacks: Change is rarely linear. Maintain your conviction while adapting your approach when you hit obstacles.

When you lead with conviction, you don't just make individual decisions based on your values—you help create a team culture where those values are lived out collectively.

Creating Values-Driven Culture:

Model the values consistently: Your team watches what you do more than what you say. Live your values visibly and consistently.

Hire and promote based on values fit: Bring people onto the team who share your core principles, not just technical skills.

Make values part of decision-making: Regularly reference your team values when making decisions and encourage others to do the same.

Recognize values-based behavior: Celebrate when team members demonstrate your shared values, especially when it requires courage or sacrifice.

Address values violations: When someone acts contrary to team values, address it quickly and directly. Values without consequences become meaningless.

Tell values stories: Share examples of team members living out your values to reinforce their importance and show what they look like in practice.

Navigating Conflicting Values and Priorities

Real leadership often involves navigating situations where multiple values or stakeholders are in conflict. Conviction doesn't mean choosing sides—it means finding solutions that honor the most important principles while acknowledging competing concerns.

Framework for Values Conflicts

Identify all stakeholders: Who is affected by this decision? What are their legitimate interests and concerns?

Clarify competing values: What principles are in tension? Are there ways to honor multiple values simultaneously?

Look for creative solutions: Can you find approaches that address multiple concerns rather than forcing an either/or choice?

Prioritize based on impact: When you must choose, which values or stakeholders have the greatest need or vulnerability?

Communicate transparently: Explain your reasoning and acknowledge the trade-offs you're making. People can accept difficult decisions when they understand the thinking behind them.

Learn and adjust: Use the experience to refine your decision-making process for future values conflicts.

Conviction in Crisis Leadership

Crisis moments reveal character and test conviction. When everything is uncertain and pressure is intense, conviction-driven leaders provide the stability and direction that teams need to navigate through difficulty.

Crisis Leadership Principles

Stay grounded in values: When everything else is changing, your principles become the anchor that keeps you steady.

Communicate frequently and honestly: People need more information during crisis, not less. Share what you know, acknowledge what you don't know, and explain how you're making decisions.

Focus on what you can control: Crisis often involves factors outside your influence. Channel your energy toward areas where your actions can make a difference.

Take care of people first: In crisis, your team's well-being should be your primary concern. Address their safety, security, and basic needs before worrying about business outcomes.

Make decisions with incomplete information: Crisis doesn't wait for perfect information. Use your values to guide decisions when data is limited or conflicting.

Learn and adapt quickly: Crisis requires rapid learning and adjustment. Stay committed to your principles while adapting your methods as you learn what works.

The Long-Term Impact of Conviction Leadership

When you consistently lead with conviction, several things happen over time:

Increased trust: People learn they can count on you to do what you say and stand up for what's right, even when it's difficult.

Clear expectations: Your team knows what you value and can predict how you'll respond in different situations.

Ripple effect: Your principled leadership influences others to also lead with conviction.

Decision-making efficiency: When your values are clear, decisions become faster because you have a framework for evaluation.

Talent attraction: People who share your values are drawn to work with you, while those who don't align tend to self-select out.

Organizational legacy: Conviction-driven leaders create lasting change that extends beyond their tenure.

Conviction is a powerful leadership tool, but it can also create problems when misapplied, including:

Rigidity: Confusing methods with principles and becoming inflexible about approaches.

Self-righteousness: Using conviction as a weapon to judge or exclude others rather than a compass for your own behavior.

Isolation: Making decisions without input from others because you believe your convictions are sufficient.

Perfectionism: Setting impossibly high standards based on your values and creating unrealistic expectations for yourself and others.

Burnout: Trying to fight every battle and stand up for every principle without prioritizing or pacing yourself.

Warning Signs of Conviction Gone Wrong

- People stop bringing you different perspectives
- You find yourself in frequent conflicts over methods rather than principles
- Team members seem afraid to challenge your ideas
- You feel exhausted from constant battles
- You're making decisions without seeking input from others

Developing Your Conviction Capacity

Leading with conviction is a skill that can be developed with practice and reflection:

Clarify your values: Spend time identifying and articulating what you truly believe in. Write them down and review them regularly.

Practice in small situations: Look for opportunities to act on your values in low-stakes situations to build your conviction muscle.

Seek feedback: Ask trusted colleagues whether your actions align with your stated values. Are there gaps they can help you see?

Study other conviction leaders: Learn from leaders you admire. How do they balance firmness with flexibility? What can you learn from their approach?

Reflect on your decisions: After making values-based decisions, analyze what worked, what didn't, and what you learned for next time.

Build your support network: Surround yourself with people who share your values and will support you when conviction requires courage.

Conviction as a Leadership Legacy

Ultimately, leading with conviction is about creating a legacy that extends beyond your immediate results. It's about standing for something bigger than yourself and inspiring others to do the same.

When you lead with conviction, you don't just achieve business outcomes—you influence how people think about leadership, ethics, and the role of values in professional life. You show others that it's possible to be successful while maintaining integrity, to be strong while remaining humble, and to stand for principles while staying open to learning.

That's the power of conviction in presence-driven leadership. It's not about being perfect or having all the answers. It's about knowing what you stand for and having the courage to act on those beliefs, even when it's difficult.

CHAPTER 6

Real World Leadership Lessons

Leadership development often happens in classrooms and workshops, but real leadership is forged in the moments when things go wrong. It's in the mistakes we make, the challenges we face, and in our response to both that we discover what kind of leaders we really are.

This chapter shares three critical leadership lessons from my career, each tied back to the Coach-Influence-Conviction framework. These aren't success stories from the start. They're stories about presence-driven leadership emerging from difficult situations, failed first attempts, and the humbling experience of learning that leadership is as much about how you handle mistakes as how you achieve victories.

Each story illustrates a different aspect of presence-driven leadership: the importance of authenticity and accountability, the power of relationship-building and empathy, and the courage required to stand for what's right even when it's unpopular. More importantly, each demonstrates that presence-driven leadership isn't about being perfect. It's about being real, responsive, and committed to growing from every experience.

Lesson 1: The Golf Maintenance Misstep and the Power of Authentic Accountability

The first significant mistake I made was when I was a new Human Resources Director (HRD) and a first-time executive committee member. I made it a point to go to all of the department stand-up meetings to introduce myself and get to know the teams. At the Golf Maintenance Team meeting, I said something that upset the team. I don't recall what it was, but what I vividly remember was that I had barely made it back to my office when a call came in to my HR coordinator to let her know about the upsetting comment I had made.

It was not my intention to say something negative. I remember thinking that what they were saying I said was slightly off from what I thought I had said. But here's the thing about leadership: your intent doesn't matter as much as your impact. When people are hurt or offended by something you said, explaining what you "really meant" doesn't heal the damage. It often makes it worse.

I had a choice to make. I could defend myself, correct the misunderstanding, and explain what I actually said, or I could focus on the relationship and the trust that had been damaged. I could make it about being right, or I could make it about being a leader.

The very next day, I went back to their meeting. I knew that this was an all-male, Hispanic team. They had been unionized but had recently decertified and voted the union out, which is very rare to do. I knew that this issue was about pride and honor. They were looking to see if I was going to be another senior leader who abuses power or not.

At that meeting, rather than defending and correcting what I said, I told the team that it was brought to my attention that they were concerned about something I said. I apologized for the concern my comments caused. I reiterated that my primary role was to be an advocate for all team members. I assured them that this was what I was there to accomplish.

I told them, "My door is always open, and you will always hear the truth from me, whether it's good or something that I think you may not want to hear. You will always know where you stand with me."

Needless to say, I convinced 90%, if not 99% of the team that I was their advocate and a servant leader that day. I never had any issues with them after and was often invited to their departmental celebrations.

The Coach-Influence-Conviction Framework in Action

This situation illustrates all three pillars of presence-driven leadership:

Coaching: Instead of lecturing the team about what I "really" meant, I created space for them to express their concerns and demonstrated that I was willing to learn from their feedback.

Influence: I could have used my position to dismiss their concerns or demand they accept my explanation. Instead, I built influence by showing vulnerability and commitment to their success.

Conviction: My core value of serving team members guided my response. I was willing to be uncomfortable and admit fault because that served the larger principle of building trust and relationships.

Key Leadership Lessons:

Impact matters more than intent: When you hurt someone, focus on the damage done, not the explanation for why you did it.

Authenticity builds trust faster than perfection: The team didn't need me to be flawless. They needed me to be real and accountable.

Cultural awareness requires humility: Understanding the cultural dynamics at play (pride, honor, and past experiences with leadership) was crucial to responding appropriately.

Quick response prevents lasting damage: Waiting would have allowed the hurt to fester and the story to grow. Immediate action demonstrated that their concerns mattered.

Vulnerability can be a strength: Admitting fault and showing genuine concern for their feelings actually increased my credibility rather than diminishing it.

Lesson 2: The New Jersey Challenge and the Power of Human Connection

Another difficult situation arose when I became the area HRD. I moved from California to New Jersey. While leadership competencies remained the same in both sites, there was a significant difference between the East Coast and West Coast.

There was a cultural dynamic with the workforce in Palm Springs, the site where I first became an HR practitioner. At that site, I worked with three main cultural work groups— distinct communities of employees who often shared a common cultural background. In New Jersey, there were more than a dozen cultural groups, which was wonderful from my perspective. This was not an issue, other than making sure I knew how to connect and engage with all team members.

The challenge I faced in New Jersey was that a few individuals were trying to unionize my home property. I had just arrived, not knowing any of the staff. The general manager was new to this property as well, having only arrived a couple of months before I did.

I had to get up to speed quickly to learn the abilities of our leadership team, the workforce, the real problems happening at this hotel, and why individuals were seeking a third party for assistance.

The general manager and I identified some main issues with pay, a shortfall in tools and equipment, and recognition, which we shored up. This was extremely helpful, but what I believe got us over the goal line was learning more about the team members.

As it turns out, one of the main folks who was speaking with the union had a slip and fall on property. As I normally would, I completed the regular administrative work to get this person on to workers' compensation. As a general practice, I work quickly to support this person in returning to work with ease.

I helped this person who did not speak very much English, and while my Spanish was rudimentary at best, I got them to their appointments and physical therapy, driving them 45 minutes to and from their sessions. It was not my normal practice to drive employees to appointments but, in this case, I saw it as an opportunity to get to know them.

During that time, I never spoke about the hotel issues. Instead, I only spent time getting to know this person's family. I opened up to them about me and my family. This person never missed any time from work, got reimbursed for their medical bills through workers' compensation, and I took the time to explain how things worked along the way.

During that time, this person sent me a Facebook friend request. If there was something they were not happy about, I heard from them. I heard from them about the good things. The unionization matter never even got to a card count. Nine years later, I got a new social media friend request from this person, and we keep in touch.

The Coach-Influence-Conviction Framework in Action

Coaching: Rather than seeing this person as an adversary to be defeated, I saw them as someone who needed support and understanding. I coached them through the workers' compensation process and helped them navigate a system they didn't fully understand.

Influence: I didn't try to argue against unionization or convince them they were wrong. Instead, I demonstrated through my actions that leadership cared about their well-being and success.

Conviction: My core value of treating people with dignity and respect guided every interaction. I was willing to invest significant personal time because I believed in serving team members, especially during difficult times.

Key Leadership Lessons:

Address systems issues first: We identified and fixed legitimate problems with pay, tools, and recognition. You can't relationship your way out of systemic problems.

Invest in individual relationships: While systems matter, personal connections often determine whether people trust leadership's intentions.

Show up during difficult times: Anyone can be supportive when things are going well. Real relationships are built when you help people through challenges.

Cultural competence requires effort: My willingness to communicate in Spanish, even imperfectly, demonstrated respect for this person's background and experience.

Consistency builds trust: Following through on workers' compensation processes and keeping commitments showed that my support was genuine, not manipulative.

Small gestures have big impact: Driving to appointments wasn't required but it created space for authentic relationship building that changed everything.

Listen more than you speak: During those car rides, I learned about family, values, and concerns that I never would have discovered in a formal meeting.

Lesson 3: Leading Through Crisis While Building DEI Infrastructure

Perhaps the most complex leadership challenge I faced during the course of my career came when I joined Atelier Ace in July 2020. The company was navigating multiple simultaneous crises, and I walked into what could only be described as a perfect storm.

I joined during the height of social unrest following the murders of Breonna Taylor, Ahmaud Arbery, George Floyd and so many others. The company had posted a Black Lives Matter solidarity statement, which created backlash both internally from some employees (and, in some cases, former employees) and externally from community members and customers who questioned whether the company genuinely believed that Black lives mattered.

Meanwhile, the pandemic was raging. We were in the process of closing properties both permanently and temporarily, reopening hotels for business, and working on future hotels under construction. The leadership teams at the properties were doing the best they could to manage the situation with customers and guests while having the senior leadership team scrutinizing their every move.

The property leaders felt that the internal corporate team was unfairly criticizing them, while the public was wrongfully accusing them of not supporting Black employees. What the public didn't know was that the hotel receiving the most criticism actually had the highest level of Black leadership managing that property, and that they were doing everything they could under incredibly difficult circumstances.

Everyone was on edge, and we were all remote, so I couldn't do the type of face-to-face meetings that would normally be essential for this kind of situation since we couldn't travel.

I was making decisions on findings from a third-party team that had conducted investigations into the various claims being made. At the same time, I was tasked with building out HR and DEI infrastructure for the entire organization during this crisis.

Rather than trying to defend or explain away the concerns, I focused on listening and building systems that would create lasting change:

Listening sessions: I conducted listening circles and sessions with internal employees to understand their experiences and concerns. This wasn't about defending the company but about genuinely hearing what people were experiencing.

Investigation follow-up: I wrapped up the third-party investigations, making decisions based on findings rather than assumptions or public pressure.

Infrastructure building: Even during the crisis, I implemented a Supplier Diversity Program before the end of 2020 and began building comprehensive DEI training programs that the company had never had before.

Training and development: We rolled out a "leaders leading inclusive teams training" and an "inclusive hiring training" to give leaders practical tools for creating inclusive environments.

Communication platform: I established regular communication channels to keep everyone informed and connected during the remote work period.

Property visits: As soon as it was safe to travel, I visited all hotels to provide in-person support and training.

The Coach-Influence-Conviction Framework in Action

Coaching: Instead of lecturing people about what they should think or feel, I created space for honest conversations and provided training that built actual capabilities for inclusive leadership.

Influence: I couldn't mandate that people change their hearts and minds, but I could build systems and processes that demonstrated the company's genuine commitment to inclusion and equity.

Conviction: My core belief in the dignity and value of all people guided every decision, even when it would have been easier to take shortcuts or avoid difficult conversations.

Key Leadership Lessons:

Multiple crises require steady leadership: When everything is chaotic, people need leaders who can stay grounded in principles while adapting to rapidly changing circumstances.

Systems change requires patience: Building lasting inclusion takes time and systematic effort, not just public statements or quick fixes.

Context matters in crisis communication: Understanding what property leaders were actually dealing with was crucial to providing appropriate support rather than additional pressure.

Infrastructure building during crisis sets the foundation for future success: The work we did during this difficult period created the systems that would serve the organization for years to come.

Listen before you lead: In emotionally charged situations, people need to feel heard before they'll trust your leadership.

Results speak louder than intentions: Ultimately, our engagement survey results showed that our DEI indices and engagement indices were all above benchmarks, and our Black employees were the most engaged of all segments.

The Outcome

What started as a crisis became an opportunity to build something stronger. By focusing on genuine listening, systematic infrastructure building, and consistent follow-through, we created an environment where people felt valued and engaged. The property leaders who had felt caught in the middle became advocates for the changes we implemented because they saw how it improved their teams and their ability to lead effectively.

This experience taught me that leading through crisis requires conviction about your values, the influence to build coalitions even when people disagree, and the coaching mindset to help people grow through difficult circumstances rather than simply demanding compliance.

These experiences taught me that presence-driven leadership isn't about having all the answers or never making mistakes. It's about how you show up when things go wrong, how you respond to challenges, and how you build relationships even in difficult circumstances.

Common Themes Across All Situations:

Authenticity over image management: In each case, being real and vulnerable was more powerful than trying to maintain a perfect leadership image.

Relationship building as foundation: Whether dealing with team concerns or union organizing, the quality of relationships determined the outcome more than policies or procedures.

Cultural competence matters: Understanding the cultural dynamics and showing respect for different perspectives was crucial in every situation.

Systems and relationships both matter: You need to address legitimate operational issues while also building personal connections and trust.

Quick response prevents escalation: In each case, immediate action and attention prevented small issues from becoming major problems.

Values guide decisions: Having clear principles about serving others and treating people with dignity provided the compass for navigating complex situations.

These stories offer practical insights you can apply in your own leadership situations:

When you make a mistake:
- Focus on impact, not intent
- Respond quickly and directly
- Take responsibility without making excuses
- Demonstrate changed behavior, not just changed words

When facing resistance or conflict:
- Look for legitimate underlying concerns
- Invest time in understanding different perspectives
- Build relationships before trying to solve problems
- Address both systems issues and relationship issues

When cultural dynamics are involved:
- Show respect through effort, not just words
- Learn about the communities you serve
- Understand that pride and honor may be at stake
- Demonstrate cultural humility and willingness to learn

When principles are tested:
- Stay grounded in your core values
- Be willing to invest personal time and effort
- Focus on long-term relationship building
- Trust that authentic care will be recognized and reciprocated

Each of these situations had an impact far beyond the immediate problem. The golf maintenance team became advocates who shared their positive experience with other departments. The New Jersey team member became a long-term connection who provided honest feedback and helped prevent future issues. The relationships built during these challenges created a foundation of trust that served the organization for years.

This is the power of presence-driven leadership. When you lead with authenticity, empathy, and conviction, you don't just solve immediate problems. You create a culture where people trust leadership, feel valued and heard, and are willing to work through challenges together rather than seeking outside intervention.

These weren't perfect leadership moments, but they were real leadership moments. And in the end, that's what makes all the difference.

CHAPTER 7

Building Team Culture Without Titles

Many leaders feel that they are restricted in their ability to create the culture they want, especially when they lack formal authority over all stakeholders. They look at organizational charts and resource limitations and conclude that culture building is something that happens at higher levels with bigger budgets and more authority.

But here's what I've learned in every leadership role I've held: culture isn't built by titles or budgets. It's built by leaders who understand that their primary job is to serve their team and remove obstacles that prevent people from doing their best work.

For me, leadership is all about being a servant leader. You need to get to know your team personally, and you need to make time for them to get to know you. Make space and set aside time in group settings and one-on-ones for this crucial step.

This chapter is about how to build strong team culture regardless of your position in the hierarchy. It's about tools for managers who feel underpowered, strategies for knocking down roadblocks, and the importance of getting to know your team deeply while modeling the respect and consistency that creates psychological safety.

The Foundation: Getting to Know Your Team (And Letting Them Know You)

Early on, I learned that one of the most disruptive parts of a team member's work experience is when a new boss comes in. Team members aren't concerned if I know state employment law or how to use the latest human resources information system (HRIS). They are much more concerned with whether the new boss cares about them.

Spend more time getting to know your team rather than trying to make a statement or name for yourself. Learn what motivates your team, their aspirations, and learn how they feel seen.

The first activity that I went through with a new team came from something my kids created for me. My kids gave me a jar of "Dad-isms" for Father's Day. "Dad-isms" are dad sayings, things I say often. Like "Are you going to sleep the whole day away?" or "Do a good job in school."

With my team, I went through that jar explaining each "Dad-ism" and the reasoning behind them. I also showed my colleagues pictures of my last team and a few work-related outings we took together. I wanted my new team to know more about me. I also asked questions about them and their roles before giving direction. This approach accomplished several things:

It humanized me: Instead of being the new authority figure, I became a real person with a family, values, and quirks.

It showed vulnerability: Sharing personal sayings and family stories demonstrated that I was willing to be authentic rather than hide behind a professional facade.

It demonstrated care for teams: Showing pictures from previous teams proved that I invest in relationships and value the people I work with.

It established dialogue: By asking about them before giving direction, I showed that I valued their input and wanted to understand their perspectives.

When I was an HRD, anytime I had a new manager join our team, I encouraged them to establish personal connections with their team members. The ones that got to know their teams fared well, and the ones who didn't had a much tougher time and often failed at that property.

This isn't just about being friendly. It's about understanding that leadership effectiveness is built on relationship foundation. When people trust you as a person, they're more likely to follow you as a leader.

Building team culture requires intentional space for people to connect as humans, not just as role-players in an organizational chart. Leverage group settings and one-on-ones to strengthen connections.

Group Settings

Team meetings with personal check-ins: Start meetings with a few minutes for people to share something going on in their lives, a recent success, or something they're looking forward to.

Shared meals: Food creates natural opportunities for conversation. Whether it's team lunches, breakfast meetings, or just bringing snacks to meetings, eating together builds bonds.

Celebration rituals: Create regular opportunities to celebrate wins, milestones, birthdays, or achievements. Make it about the people, not just the performance.

Team outings: Off-site activities, volunteer opportunities, or simple walking meetings can create different dynamics than conference room interactions.

One-on-One Settings

Regular individual meetings: Schedule consistent time with each team member, not just when there are problems to solve.

Career conversations: Ask about their goals, aspirations, and what they want to learn or develop.

Personal interests: Learn about their families, hobbies, and what they care about outside of work.

Work preferences: Understand how they like to receive feedback, what motivates them, and what conditions help them do their best work.

Challenge discussions: Create safe space for them to share frustrations, concerns, or ideas for improvement.

The Servant Leader's Primary Role: Knocking Down Roadblocks

The primary role of a servant leader is to knock down any roadblocks that prevent the team from doing their jobs. These roadblocks might look like being short-staffed or not having all the tools that they need to do their job. When you remove those obstacles, your team will thrive.

Resource Issues:
- Insufficient tools, equipment, or supplies
- Outdated technology or systems
- Inadequate workspace or facilities
- Budget constraints that prevent necessary purchases

Process Problems:
- Unclear procedures or workflows
- Redundant approvals or bureaucracy

- Poor communication between departments
- Inefficient scheduling or resource allocation

Information Gaps:
- Lack of clarity about priorities or expectations
- Missing context about decisions or changes
- Insufficient training or onboarding
- Poor communication from senior leadership

Relationship Challenges:
- Conflicts between team members or departments
- Difficult customer or stakeholder relationships
- Lack of support from other areas of the organization
- Cultural or communication barriers

The Roadblock Removal Process:

Listen actively: Regularly ask your team what's preventing them from being successful. Don't wait for annual surveys or formal feedback sessions.

Investigate thoroughly: Don't assume you understand the problem based on initial descriptions. Dig deeper to understand root causes.

Prioritize based on impact: You can't solve everything at once. Focus on obstacles that affect multiple people or prevent critical work from happening.

Use your influence strategically: Even without formal authority, you often have relationships and credibility you can leverage to address systemic issues.

Communicate progress: Let your team know what you're working on, even if you can't solve the problem immediately. Knowing you're advocating for them matters.

Find creative solutions: Sometimes you can't eliminate the roadblock but you can find workarounds or alternative approaches.

Tools for Managers Who Feel They Have Limited Authority

Many managers, especially those in middle management or matrix organizations, feel like they lack the authority to create meaningful change. Here are practical tools that work regardless of your position. Map your actual influence versus your perceived limitations:

- What decisions can you make independently?
- What changes can you implement within your team?
- Which stakeholders trust your judgment and recommendations?
- What budget or resources do you control?
- Where do you have informal influence or relationships?

Often, you have more power than you realize. The key is using it strategically. Instead of trying to solve major organizational problems, focus on incremental improvements that compound over time:

Week 1: Improve one recurring meeting by adding structure or reducing time

Week 2: Solve one persistent scheduling or communication issue

Week 3: Implement one small process improvement

Week 4: Address one team member's specific frustration or need

Small, consistent improvements build momentum and credibility for larger changes. Partner with other managers or departments who share similar challenges:

- Share resources and best practices

- Present joint proposals for system-wide improvements
- Support each other's initiatives
- Create informal networks for problem-solving

Keep track of patterns, successes, and challenges:
- Document what roadblocks come up repeatedly
- Track the impact of changes you make
- Record positive feedback from team members or customers
- Note resources or support that would make a difference

This documentation becomes valuable when you have opportunities to present ideas to senior leadership.

Creating Recognition Systems Without Budget Authority

One of the biggest culture builders is recognition, but many managers assume they need budget approval or formal programs to acknowledge good work effectively.

No-Cost Recognition Strategies:

Public acknowledgment: Use team meetings, email, or internal communications to highlight good work. Be specific about what they did and why it mattered.

Peer nomination systems: Create ways for team members to recognize each other's contributions. This builds culture while reducing the burden on you as the only source of recognition.

Skill development opportunities: Offer to let high performers attend webinars, shadow other departments, or take on stretch assignments.

Flexible work arrangements: When possible, offer schedule flexibility, remote work options, or choice in assignments as recognition for strong performance.

Access and inclusion: Invite strong performers to meetings, strategy sessions, or decision-making processes they wouldn't normally attend.

Written recommendations: Offer to write LinkedIn recommendations, performance review input, or reference letters for people who have contributed significantly.

The Key to Effective Recognition:

Be specific: Instead of "great job," say "the way you handled that difficult customer situation yesterday showed real professionalism and problem-solving skills."

Be timely: Recognize contributions soon after they happen, not months later during review cycles.

Match the person: Some people love public recognition while others prefer private acknowledgment. Learn what each person values.

Focus on impact: Connect their work to larger goals, customer satisfaction, or team success.

Culture is created more by what leaders' model than what they mandate. Your team watches how you treat people, how you handle stress, and how you respond to challenges.

Daily Behaviors That Build Culture:

Consistent communication style: Treat everyone with the same level of respect and professionalism, regardless of their position or how well you know them.

Follow-through on commitments: When you say you'll do something, do it. When you can't, communicate proactively and explain why.

Transparent decision-making: When possible, explain the reasoning behind decisions, especially ones that affect the team.

Calm under pressure: Your emotional regulation sets the tone for how the team handles stress and challenges.

Inclusive participation: Make sure everyone has opportunities to contribute ideas and feedback, not just the most vocal team members.

Accountability with dignity: When performance issues arise, address them directly but respectfully, focusing on behavior and impact rather than character.

Continuous learning: Admit when you don't know something, ask for input, and show that you're willing to change based on new information.

Building Psychological Safety at the Team Level

Psychological safety is the foundation of strong team culture. It's the belief that you can speak up, ask questions, make mistakes, and be vulnerable without fear of negative consequences.

Normalize mistakes: When someone makes an error, focus on learning and prevention rather than blame and punishment.

Ask for feedback: Regularly ask for input about your leadership and team processes. Act on what you hear.

Admit your own mistakes: When you mess up, acknowledge it quickly and focus on what you learned.

Encourage questions: Make it clear that questions are welcome, especially during training or when introducing new processes.

Address conflict directly: Don't let interpersonal issues fester. Create safe spaces for people to work through disagreements.

Celebrate different perspectives: When someone offers a different viewpoint, acknowledge the value before discussing the merits.

Building culture is not a one-time initiative. It requires consistent attention and reinforcement over time.

Monthly Culture Check-ins:
- What's working well on our team right now?
- What's getting in the way of our success?
- How can we better support each other?
- What would make this a more enjoyable place to work?

Quarterly Team Reflection:
- How have we grown as a team this quarter?
- What challenges have we overcome together?
- What do we want to focus on improving next quarter?
- How can we celebrate our progress?

Annual Culture Assessment:
- What are we most proud of as a team?
- Where do we still have opportunities to improve?
- How has our culture contributed to our results?
- What do we want to be known for as a team?

The Ripple Effect of Team Culture

When you build strong culture within your team, the impact extends beyond your immediate group:

Other teams notice: Strong team culture becomes a model that other groups want to emulate.

Talent attraction: People want to work with teams that have reputations for being supportive and effective.

Customer impact: Teams with strong culture provide better service and create better experiences for customers.

Organizational influence: Senior leadership notices teams that consistently perform well and have high engagement.

Leadership development: Team members from strong cultures often become effective leaders themselves, spreading the approach throughout the organization.

Remember, you don't need permission or perfect authority to start building the culture you want. You just need the commitment to serve your team, remove obstacles, and create an environment where people can do their best work.

That's how presence-driven leaders create change from wherever they are, regardless of what their title says they are expected to do.

CHAPTER 8

Leading Through Crisis and Change

Crisis doesn't announce itself. It arrives suddenly, disrupts everything you thought you knew, and tests every leadership principle you've ever learned. The comfortable routines disappear, the familiar structures shift, and everyone looks to leaders for stability in an unstable world.

This chapter is about leading through those moments when the ground falls out beneath you. It's about maintaining your presence when everything around you is changing, supporting your team through uncertainty, and making difficult decisions with humanity. Most importantly, it's about understanding that crisis reveals character and that how you show up during the hardest times defines your leadership legacy.

The stories in this chapter come from real crisis moments in my career: management contract losses that forced painful restructuring, layoffs that affected me personally, and relentless pressure that pushed teams to their breaking point. Each situation taught me something different about what it means to lead with presence when presence is exactly what people need most.

When our company lost a few hotel management agreements, it forced us to face hard truths about leadership transitions. Suddenly, the financial performance was taking a significant hit and the CEO wanted to bring in a COO. It was a period full of uncertainty and shifting roles but what stood out to me was how people clung to their turf.

A management contract is an agreement between a hotel owner and a management company to operate their property on the owner's behalf. The management company handles everything from daily operations to strategic planning, typically earning fees based on the property's performance. Losing management contracts in hospitality isn't just about revenue. It's about identity, relationships, and the future of teams who have poured their energy into making properties successful. When those contracts disappear, everything gets questioned: strategy, leadership, structure, and individual roles.

The financial pressure was immediate and intense. Leadership was under scrutiny from ownership and investors. The decision to bring in a COO created additional anxiety because existing leaders worried about their relevance and security in the new structure.

What struck me most during this period was how quickly people shifted into self-preservation mode. Leaders who had previously collaborated became territorial. Information sharing decreased as people worried about protecting their positions. Energy that should have been focused on serving customers and supporting teams got redirected toward internal politics and positioning.

This is a natural human response to organizational crisis but it's also destructive. When leaders are focused on protecting themselves, they can't effectively serve their teams or customers.

My role became helping the team navigate that insecurity, even when I was not 100% sold about the structure. I had to be a steady presence, focused on the long-term culture, rather than getting pulled into the swirl of self-preservation.

This required several key leadership choices:

Acknowledge the uncertainty honestly: I didn't pretend everything was fine or that I had answers I didn't have. People can sense when leaders are being dishonest about challenges, and false optimism destroys credibility.

Focus on what we could control: While we couldn't control market conditions or ownership decisions, we could control how we supported each other and served our teams.

Model collaboration rather than competition: Instead of protecting my own territory, I looked for ways to help other leaders succeed and find their footing in the new structure.

Keep the long-term perspective: Rather than getting caught up in daily drama and positioning, I focused on building culture and relationships that would serve the organization regardless of structural changes.

Support the transition even when uncertain: Leadership sometimes requires supporting decisions you're not completely sure about while working to make them successful rather than undermining them.

Key Lessons from Leadership Transitions:

Crisis amplifies existing cultural problems: If people don't trust each other during good times, they definitely won't trust each other during crisis.

Leaders set the emotional tone: Your team takes cues from how you respond to uncertainty. If you're panicked or territorial, they will be too.

Transparency builds trust: People can handle difficult truth better than they can handle being kept in the dark.

Focus energy on service, not survival: Teams that maintain their focus on serving customers and each other perform better during transitions.

Change is constant; character is choice: You can't control what happens to your organization but you can control how you respond.

Layoffs always hit me hard but, in this case, it happened to me. I was the only VP out of six who was cut, and while I suspected age may have played a factor, I chose to handle it with dignity.

Being laid off when you're in a senior leadership position carries unique challenges. You're supposed to be the one providing stability and direction to others, yet suddenly you're the one whose future is uncertain. The temptation to become bitter, defensive, or to lash out is real and understandable.

I had seen others navigate layoffs poorly, clinging to bitterness or burning bridges. I made a different choice.

I knew how painful it was for the people who stayed, so I approached it with humanity, letting my team know they would be okay and modeling calm when they needed it most.

This choice wasn't easy. Even though my email was shut off and the transition wasn't handled with much grace behind the scenes from what I was told firsthand, I carried myself with presence.

Why This Choice Mattered:

For my team: They were watching to see how I would handle this crisis. If I fell apart or became bitter, it would increase their anxiety about their own security and the organization's future.

For my reputation: How you handle setbacks becomes part of your leadership story. People remember how you respond when things go wrong more than how you celebrate when things go right.

For my own integrity: Leading with presence isn't just about when you have formal authority. It's about who you are as a person, regardless of your title or circumstances.

For the organization: Even though I was leaving, I could either contribute to healing or add to the damage. I chose to help the organization move forward rather than create additional problems.

Practical Strategies for Leading Through Personal Crisis:

Separate your identity from your role: You are not your job title. Your worth and capabilities exist independent of any particular position.

Focus on your team's needs: When you're dealing with your own crisis, serving others can provide purpose and perspective.

Control what you can control: You can't control organizational decisions but you can control your response and the energy you bring to interactions.

Model the behavior you want to see: If you want people to handle change with grace, you need to demonstrate what that looks like.

Maintain long-term perspective: This crisis will pass. How you handle it will affect relationships and opportunities for years to come.

That moment reinforced my belief that leadership is about how you show up when the ground falls out beneath you.

At one particular hotel, there was a stretch when the owner's demands were relentless, the leadership team was being cut, and the benefits open enrollment process was overwhelming the leaders. In particular, my GM and HRD were exhausted, and I could hear it in every conversation we had.

Some periods in business feel like everything is happening at once. External pressures mount, internal resources are stretched, and teams reach their breaking points. During these times, leaders can feel isolated and overwhelmed, questioning whether they can handle the demands being placed on them.

This particular situation combined multiple stressors:
- Unrealistic owner expectations and demands
- Staff reductions that increased workload for remaining team members
- Complex administrative processes happening during an already difficult time
- Leadership team members who were emotionally and physically exhausted

I stayed close to them, texting and calling almost daily, letting them vent, coaching them through the pressure, and making sure they didn't feel alone and were being heard and helping with solutions.

Daily Support Strategies:

Regular check-ins: Instead of waiting for scheduled meetings, I reached out proactively to see how they were doing and what support they needed.

Safe space for venting: Sometimes people need to express frustration and stress before they can problem-solve. I provided that outlet without judgment.

Active listening: I focused on understanding their experience rather than immediately jumping to solutions or minimizing their concerns.

Coaching through pressure: I helped them think through specific challenges and develop strategies for managing competing demands.

Solution-oriented support: While I provided emotional support, I also worked with them to identify concrete actions that could improve their challenges.

Validation and encouragement: I acknowledged the difficulty of their situation and reminded them of their capabilities and past successes.

The Impact of Presence During Crisis:

Reduced isolation: Knowing that someone understands and cares about the obstacles that they're facing helps leaders feel less alone in their challenges.

Improved decision-making: When people feel supported, they can think more clearly and make better choices under pressure.

Increased resilience: Regular support builds emotional reserves that help people handle ongoing stress.

Maintained performance: Teams that feel supported by their leaders are more likely to maintain quality and service standards during difficult periods.

Enhanced loyalty: People remember who showed up for them during their hardest times.

Framework for Crisis Communication

Crisis communication requires a different approach than normal business communication. People need more information, more frequently, delivered with greater empathy and clarity.

The CLEAR Framework for Crisis Communication:

(C)ommunicate frequently: During crisis, people need more information than usual. Even when you don't have updates, check in to see how people are doing.

(L)isten actively: Pay attention to what people are saying and what they're not saying. Watch for signs of stress, confusion, or disengagement.

(E)mphasize what you know: Be clear about facts while acknowledging uncertainty. People can handle ambiguity better when they understand what is certain.

(A)cknowledge emotions: Crisis creates real emotional responses. Recognizing and validating those feelings builds trust and connection.

(R)einforce values and priorities: When everything else is changing, remind people of the principles and purposes that remain constant.

During restructuring at a company where I once worked, I learned that effective crisis communication isn't about having all the answers. It's about maintaining trust when everything feels uncertain. Be honest about what you don't know—credibility comes from truthfulness, not from pretending to have answers you don't have. Focus on the impact on people by explaining how changes will affect individuals and teams, not just the organization. Provide context for decisions to help people understand the reasoning behind difficult choices, even when they don't like the outcomes. Create opportunities for questions and make it easy for people to get clarification and express concerns. Most importantly, follow up on commitments. If you say you'll find out something or take a specific action, do it. Trust is built through consistent follow-through.

Crisis often requires leaders to make decisions that negatively affect people they care about. The key is making those decisions in ways that preserve dignity and maintain relationships, even when the outcomes are painful.

Involve people in the process when possible: When you can't control the outcome, give people input into how the process unfolds.

Provide as much notice as possible: Don't surprise people with decisions that affect their lives unless absolutely necessary.

Explain the reasoning: Help people understand why difficult decisions were made, even if they disagree with them.

Offer support for transitions: Provide resources, connections, or assistance to help people navigate changes.

Maintain respect throughout: Treat people with dignity regardless of the circumstances. How you handle difficult conversations affects everyone who witnesses them.

Follow through on commitments: If you promise references, transition support, or other assistance, deliver on those promises.

Building Organizational Resilience

Organizations that navigate a crisis well have built resilience before the crisis hits. This resilience comes from strong relationships, clear values, and practiced leadership skills. Specifically, teams that trust each other and their leaders handle crisis better than those with weak relationship bonds. When people understand what the organization stands for, they can make good decisions even when specific guidance isn't available. Organizations where leadership skills are developed throughout the hierarchy are more adaptable during crisis. Teams that regularly share information and discuss challenges are better prepared for crisis communication. Organizations that treat setbacks as learning opportunities recover faster and emerge stronger. Strong foundational practices provide more options during a crisis and reduce the severity of necessary changes.

Leading through crisis is emotionally and physically demanding. Sustainable crisis leadership requires attention to your own well-being and resilience. Leaders should maintain perspective by remembering that most crises are temporary. Focus on the long-term rather than getting overwhelmed by immediate pressures. Take care of your physical health. Sleep, exercise, and nutrition become more important during stress, not less important. Build your support network. Have people you can talk to honestly about the challenges you're facing. Don't try to handle everything alone. Give yourself grace because you will make mistakes and have difficult days. Treat yourself with the same kindness you would show others. Focus on what you can control by channeling your energy toward areas where your actions can make a difference rather than worrying about factors outside your influence. Don't compromise your principles because of pressure. Leading with integrity becomes more important during crisis, not less important.

Here's what took me time to understand: while crisis is painful and disruptive, it also creates opportunities for growth, change, and strengthened relationships. The key is maintaining enough presence and perspective to recognize and act on those opportunities.

At the company, the crisis forced conversations we'd been avoiding, clarified priorities we'd been debating, and brought out capabilities in people that might never have emerged otherwise. Crisis breaks down resistance to necessary changes that were difficult to implement during stable times. Shared challenges often bring people closer together and build deeper trust. Crisis shows you what people are really capable of when they're pushed beyond their comfort zones. When resources are limited, it becomes easier to identify what really matters and eliminate what doesn't. Successfully navigating crisis builds confidence and capability for handling future challenges, and it creates opportunities for emerging leaders to step up and for experienced leaders to develop new skills.

The goal of crisis leadership isn't just to survive difficult times. It's to emerge stronger, more resilient, and better prepared for future challenges.

Characteristics of Teams That Emerge Stronger:

They learned from the experience: They took time to reflect on what worked, what didn't, and what they want to do differently in the future.

They strengthened relationships: The crisis brought people closer together rather than driving them apart.

They developed new capabilities: They discovered strengths and skills they didn't know they had.

They clarified their values: The experience helped them understand what really matters and what they're willing to fight for.

They built better systems: They used the crisis as an opportunity to fix problems and improve processes.

They increased their confidence: Having successfully navigated crisis, they feel more prepared for future challenges.

Remember, crisis leadership isn't about being perfect or having all the answers. It's about showing up with presence, making decisions with humanity, and supporting your team through uncertainty. When you lead this way, you don't just survive crisis. You use it as an opportunity to become the leader your team needs and to build an organization that can thrive regardless of what challenges lie ahead.

CHAPTER 9

Presence in Today's Workplace

The fundamentals of presence-driven leadership remain constant but the context in which we lead has transformed dramatically. The modern workplace looks nothing like the organizations where traditional leadership models were developed. We're leading across distances, through screens, and with generational expectations that challenge many long-held assumptions about work and leadership.

This chapter explores how the Coach-Influence-Conviction framework adapts to modern realities while maintaining its core principles. Whether you're leading hybrid teams, navigating digital communication, or engaging with multi-generational workforces, presence-driven leadership provides a foundation that transcends specific technologies or workplace arrangements.

The key insight is this: presence isn't about physical proximity or formal authority. It's about authentic connection, genuine care for people's growth, and consistent demonstration of your values. These qualities translate across industries, communication platforms, and generational preferences when applied with intentionality and adaptation.

While my experience is rooted in hospitality, the Coach-Influence-Conviction framework applies across industries because it addresses universal human needs: people want to be developed, to have influence in their work, and to be led by people with clear values.

Technology Sector Application

In fast-paced technology environments, presence-driven leadership addresses the challenge of maintaining human connection amid rapid change and technical complexity.

Coaching in tech means helping engineers and developers think through complex problems rather than providing technical solutions. It's asking, "What approaches have you considered?" instead of "Here's how to code this."

Influence in tech requires credibility through understanding business impact, not just technical expertise. Leaders who can translate technical work into business value gain influence across the organization.

Conviction in tech means standing firm on quality, user experience, or ethical considerations even when speed to market creates pressure to compromise.

Healthcare Applications

Healthcare environments demand presence-driven leadership because patient care depends on engaged, committed teams working under high pressure.

Coaching in healthcare focuses on clinical decision-making, patient interaction skills, and managing the emotional demands of caring for others.

Influence in healthcare requires building trust with medical professionals who have extensive training and strong opinions about patient care approaches.

Conviction in healthcare centers on patient safety, quality care, and ethical treatment, often requiring difficult conversations about resource constraints or protocol compliance.

Manufacturing Application

Manufacturing leadership must balance efficiency demands with safety requirements and workforce engagement.

Coaching in manufacturing involves helping supervisors develop problem-solving skills for production challenges and interpersonal skills for team management.

Influence in manufacturing requires understanding operational constraints while advocating for improvements that serve both productivity and worker well-being.

Conviction in manufacturing means never compromising on safety standards, regardless of production pressures, and maintaining quality standards even when cost reduction creates temptation to cut corners.

Financial Services Application

Financial services leadership must navigate regulatory requirements, client expectations, and performance pressures while maintaining ethical standards.

Coaching in financial services focuses on managing client relationship skills, risk assessment capabilities, and decision-making under uncertainty.

Influence in financial services requires building trust with clients, regulators, and internal stakeholders who all have different priorities and concerns.

Conviction in financial services means maintaining fiduciary responsibility and ethical standards even when competitive pressure creates incentives to compromise.

Hybrid and Remote Leadership Challenges

Leading hybrid and remote teams requires intentional adaptation of presence-driven leadership principles. The challenge isn't that these principles don't work virtually. It's that they require more deliberate application when you can't rely on informal interactions and physical presence to build relationships.

Building Coaching Relationships Remotely:

Schedule connection time: In remote environments, coaching conversations must be more intentionally scheduled rather than happening spontaneously in hallways or offices.

Video-first interactions: Coaching requires reading emotional cues and building rapport, which happens more effectively through video than audio-only calls.

Follow-up systems: Remote coaching requires more structured follow-up to ensure commitments are met and progress is tracked.

Safe space creation: Building psychological safety virtually requires explicit attention to creating confidential, judgment-free environments for coaching conversations.

Influence Across Digital Platforms:

Digital relationship building: Influence requires relationship foundation, which takes longer to build through digital communication. Leaders must invest extra time in understanding team members' perspectives and challenges.

Strategic communication: Without casual interactions, every communication becomes more intentional. Influential leaders use email, messaging, and video calls strategically to build credibility and connection.

Cross-functional collaboration: Influencing peers and stakeholders requires more structured approaches to virtual meetings, project collaboration, and information sharing.

Virtual networking: Building influence networks requires participation in virtual industry events, online communities, and digital professional relationships.

Conviction in Virtual Environments:

Values modeling: Demonstrating values through digital communication requires consistency across all platforms and interactions, from formal presentations to casual team chats.

Decision transparency: When teams can't observe daily decision-making, leaders must be more explicit about how their values guide their choices.

Cultural reinforcement: Maintaining values-driven culture requires more intentional communication about what the organization stands for and how those values apply to remote work situations.

Accountability systems: Conviction-driven accountability requires clear systems for tracking commitments and addressing performance issues when you can't rely on visual supervision.

Generational Leadership: Understanding Today's Workforce

Previously, we had more individuals in our industry driven by the potential of upward mobility. Now it's an expectation for individuals to move up regardless of experience level. This shift requires leaders to understand what motivates different generations and how to adapt their approach while maintaining consistent standards.

Debunking Millennial and Gen Z Misconceptions:

The myths about younger generations often prevent leaders from effectively engaging with them. Here are the realities:

They're lazy and entitled - In reality, they're highly motivated and driven by purpose. They seek meaningful work and will work hard when they believe in what they're doing.

They lack loyalty and frequently job-hop - In reality, they know they can find better opportunities and aren't afraid to pursue them. They invest in companies that invest in them.

They have unrealistic expectations about work-life balance - In reality, they have high expectations for thriving within life and at work. They believe it's possible to thrive in both areas simultaneously.

They're not interested in traditional career paths - In reality, they value building capabilities, making an impact, and unique development journeys rather than linear advancement.

They can't handle feedback and are overly sensitive - In reality, they crave feedback when it's real-time, constructive, and delivered with respect. They want to grow, not be micromanaged.

From research and coaching conversations, here are the traits that stand out for leading Millennials and Gen Z:

Clarity: Clear expectations, clear communication, and clear connection between their work and larger goals.

Consistency: Caring plus connected plus communication. They want leaders who demonstrate care consistently through their actions and communication.

Coaching (not Commanding): They value leaders who coach and develop their strengths rather than just assigning tasks.

Flexibility: Both in scheduling and work duties. They want options in how and when they accomplish their goals.

Purpose: Clear performance expectations combined with understanding how their role adds value to the organization and customers.

Leading Millennial and Gen Z workers isn't about lowering standards. It's about raising the bar on how we engage, connect, and communicate. The modern workforce requires empathy, flexibility, and purpose but not at the cost of clarity and transparency.

Gen Z and Millennials value leaders who coach, not coddle or micromanage. Clear support must be paired with high expectations to drive performance and engagement. Leaders who soften standards in the name of support risk eroding accountability and culture.

As I often say: "Support without standards isn't leadership. It's permission."

The best leaders set the bar *and* build the bridge. They maintain high expectations while providing the support, coaching, and development that helps people meet those expectations.

Generational Adaptation Strategies:

For Baby Boomers and Gen X team members: Respect their experience while engaging them in mentoring and knowledge transfer roles. They value stability and clear hierarchies but can adapt when they understand the business rationale.

For Millennials: Focus on collaboration, purpose, and development opportunities. They want to understand how their work contributes to larger goals and appreciate leaders who invest in their growth.

For Gen Z: Emphasize authenticity, diversity, and continuous learning. They value real-time feedback, technological fluency, and leaders who demonstrate genuine care for their development and well-being.

While adaptation is important, certain leadership principles resonate across all generations:

Respect: Everyone wants to be treated with dignity and have their contributions valued.

Growth: All generations appreciate leaders who help them develop new capabilities and advance their careers.

Purpose: People across generations want to understand how their work matters and contributes to something meaningful.

Fairness: Consistent application of standards and policies builds trust regardless of generational differences.

Communication: Clear, honest communication about expectations, feedback, and organizational changes serves everyone well.

Building Digital Presence

Digital presence isn't about mastering every new technology platform. It's about translating the authentic connection and genuine care that define presence-driven leadership through whatever communication tools your organization uses.

Authenticity through Screens:

Video presence: Use video calls to maintain face-to-face connection. Your presence comes through your attention, energy, and genuine engagement, not just your words.

Written communication: Your values and character come through in how you write emails, provide feedback, and respond to messages. Consistency across platforms builds credibility.

Digital body language: Respond promptly to messages, acknowledge receipt of important communications, and use technology in ways that demonstrate respect for others' time and priorities.

Virtual meeting leadership: Create inclusive environments in virtual meetings by ensuring everyone has opportunities to contribute and by managing technology to minimize barriers to participation.

Creating Psychological Safety Digitally:

Explicit communication: What might be implied in face-to-face interactions must be explicitly stated in digital communication. Make your support and availability clear.

Private channels: Create opportunities for confidential conversations through private video calls, phone conversations, or secure messaging platforms.

Response expectations: Set clear expectations about response times and availability to reduce anxiety about digital communication delays.

Technology equity: Ensure all team members have access to the necessary technology and training to participate fully in digital work environments.

Modern Workplace Challenges

Modern leaders face unique challenges that require adaptation of traditional leadership approaches:

Information Overload: With constant communication through multiple channels, leaders must help teams prioritize and focus on what matters most while maintaining connection and responsiveness.

Always-On Culture: The boundary between work and personal time has blurred, requiring leaders to model healthy boundaries while maintaining necessary availability and responsiveness.

Rapid Change: The pace of technological and organizational change requires leaders who can maintain stability and direction while adapting quickly to new realities.

Global Teams: Leading across time zones, cultures, and languages requires enhanced cultural competence and more structured communication approaches.

Mental Health Awareness: Modern leaders must understand the impact of work stress on mental health and create environments that support well-being alongside productivity.

Skills Obsolescence: As technology changes rapidly, leaders must help teams continuously develop new capabilities while maintaining productivity in current roles.

The Consistent Foundation

Regardless of industry, communication platform, or generational mix, presence-driven leadership provides a consistent foundation that adapts to any context:

People want to be developed: Whether in person or virtual, across all generations and industries, people appreciate leaders who invest in their growth and help them reach their potential.

Authenticity builds trust: Genuine leadership creates stronger relationships than perfect performance across all communication platforms and organizational structures.

Values provide direction: Clear principles guide decision-making and behavior regardless of changing circumstances or new challenges.

Service orientation matters: Leaders who focus on serving others and removing obstacles create engagement and loyalty in any environment.

The key is maintaining these core principles while adapting your methods to fit the realities of your specific context. Presence-driven leadership isn't a rigid framework. It's a flexible approach that honors universal human needs while adapting to changing workplace realities.

CHAPTER 10

Tools for Immediate Application

Leadership development often stops at understanding. People read about frameworks, attend workshops, and discuss principles but struggle to translate insights into sustainable practice. This chapter bridges that gap by providing a practical roadmap that integrates everything we've explored into tools you can use immediately.

The goal isn't to give you more things to remember. It's to help you weave the Coach-Influence-Conviction framework into how you already work, creating sustainable habits that build your leadership presence over time. These aren't additional tasks to add to your schedule. They're ways to approach your existing responsibilities with greater intentionality and impact.

Every tool in this chapter connects to concepts from previous chapters, showing how self-awareness, coaching, influence, conviction, culture building, crisis leadership, and modern workplace adaptation work together as an integrated approach to presence-driven leadership.

Presence-driven leadership isn't three separate skills you develop in sequence. Coach, Influence, and Conviction work together as a unified approach where each element strengthens the others.

The Self-Awareness Foundation:

Before you can effectively coach others, influence stakeholders, or lead with conviction, you need the self-awareness we explored in Chapter 2. Your ability to recognize your triggers, understand your values, and manage your emotions becomes the foundation for everything else.

When you're coaching someone through a challenge, your self-awareness helps you stay curious rather than defensive when they push back on your suggestions. When you're trying to influence a resistant stakeholder, understanding your own motivations helps you focus on their needs rather than your ego. When you're making a conviction-based decision, clarity about your values helps you act quickly and confidently.

The Daily Integration

Morning Intention Setting: Start each day by identifying which of the three pillars you want to focus on. This doesn't mean ignoring the others but having a primary intention helps you notice opportunities to practice.

Midday Check-In: Pause briefly to reflect on how you're showing up. Are you coaching through challenges or jumping to solutions? Are you building influence through relationships or relying on authority? Are your decisions reflecting your values?

Evening Reflection: End each day by noting one example of how you applied the framework and one opportunity you missed. This builds awareness without creating self-criticism.

Self-Assessment Integration

Combine the presence-driven leadership assessment from Chapter 1 with the emotional intelligence insights from Chapter 2 to create a comprehensive starting point for your development.

Every three months, complete this integrated assessment:

Presence-Driven Leadership Indicators:
- How consistently am I coaching rather than directing?
- How effectively am I influencing without relying on authority?
- How clearly are my values guiding my decisions?
- How well am I building culture regardless of my formal role?

Emotional Intelligence Application:
- How quickly am I recognizing my emotional state during difficult conversations?
- How effectively am I managing my triggers when under pressure?
- How well am I reading the emotional dynamics in team interactions?
- How consistently am I responding rather than reacting in challenging situations?

Based on your assessment, identify one specific area for development over the next quarter. Create a simple practice plan that focuses on that area without overwhelming yourself with multiple development goals.

Daily Practice Tools

The Five-Minute Coach Check:

Before any meeting or interaction where you might typically provide direction or solve problems, ask yourself:
- What if I asked questions instead of giving answers?
- How can I help this person think through the challenge?
- What would they learn if they solved this themselves?

This brief pause shifts you from manager mode to coach mode and often leads to more powerful conversations.

The Influence Inventory:

Weekly, review your influence-building activities:
- What relationships did I strengthen this week?
- How did I add value to others' success?
- Where did I build credibility through competence and character?
- What influence opportunities did I miss?

This reflection helps you see influence building as an ongoing practice rather than something that happens only when you need something.

The Values Decision Filter:

When facing any significant decision, run it through this quick filter:
- Which of my core values applies to this situation?
- What would I do if I were completely confident in my principles?
- How does this decision serve the long-term good of the team?

- What would I want other leaders to do in this situation?

This process helps you make conviction-based decisions quickly while maintaining consistency with your principles.

Crisis-Ready Leadership Tools

The real-world lessons from Chapters 6-8 provide specific tools for maintaining presence during difficult times.

The Crisis Communication Framework:
When unexpected challenges arise, use this structure:
1. **Acknowledge the reality** without minimizing or catastrophizing
2. **Express empathy** for how the situation affects people
3. **Share what you know** and what you don't know honestly
4. **Outline immediate actions** you're taking or plan to take
5. **Commit to follow-up** communication as more information becomes available

The Relationship Investment System:
Build crisis resilience by consistently investing in relationships before you need them:
- Schedule regular one-on-one time with key stakeholders.
- Offer help to colleagues who aren't asking for anything.
- Share information and resources generously.
- Acknowledge others' contributions publicly and specifically.
- Check in on people's well-being, not just their work progress.

The Values Anchor Practice:
During crisis or change, regularly remind yourself and your team of your core values:

- Start important meetings by referencing relevant values.
- Use values language when explaining difficult decisions.
- Share stories of how values guided past decisions.
- Ask team members how values apply to current challenges.
- Celebrate examples of values-driven behavior during difficult times.

Modern Application Guide

Integrate the insights from Chapter 9 into a cohesive approach for today's workplace challenges.

The Hybrid Leadership Checklist:
- For each team member, regardless of location:
- Do I understand their current challenges and priorities?
- Have I had a meaningful development conversation with them recently?
- Do they know how their work contributes to larger goals?
- Are they getting the recognition and feedback they need?
- What obstacles can I remove to help them succeed?

The Generational Adaptation Guide:

Rather than trying to remember specific approaches for each generation, focus on universal principles that resonate across age groups:

- **Clarity:** Be explicit about expectations and communication.
- **Consistency:** Demonstrate care through reliable actions and communication.
- **Coaching:** Develop their strengths rather than just assigning tasks.

- **Flexibility:** Offer options in how they achieve goals when possible.
- **Purpose:** Connect their work to meaningful outcomes.

The Digital Presence Practices:

When you're leading through Zoom, Teams, Google Meet, Slack, or any other digital platform, it's easy to lose the human element. These practices help you stay connected to your team regardless of the medium:

- Use video calls for important conversations to maintain human connection. Turn on your camera, people need to see you, not a black box with your initials.
- Respond to messages promptly to demonstrate respect and reliability.
- Be intentional about written communication tone and clarity.
- Create opportunities for informal interaction in virtual environments.
- Maintain consistent values and character across all digital platforms.

Beyond Traditional Metrics

Most organizations measure leadership effectiveness through traditional HR metrics like employee satisfaction scores, turnover rates, and performance ratings. While these matter, presence-driven leadership requires looking beyond standard metrics to track cultural health and leadership impact.

Cultural Health Indicators

Psychological Safety Measures

- How often do team members admit mistakes or ask for help?
- Do people share ideas that might be unpopular or controversial?
- How do people respond when someone disagrees with leadership?
- Are difficult conversations happening or being avoided?

Development Impact Tracking
- How many people have taken on new responsibilities or challenges?
- What percentage of internal promotions come from developed talent versus external hires?
- How often do team members coach or mentor others?
- Are people seeking more responsibility or avoiding it?

Values Alignment Assessment
- How consistently do decisions reflect stated organizational values?
- Do people reference values when explaining their choices?
- How do people talk about the organization when leadership isn't present?
- Are there examples of people choosing values over convenience?

Influence Network Analysis
- Who do people go to for advice beyond formal reporting relationships?
- How does information flow through the organization?
- Where do new ideas typically originate?

- How are conflicts typically resolved?

Leadership Pipeline Strength
- How many people are ready for increased responsibility?
- What percentage of leadership positions are filled internally?
- How effectively do current leaders develop others?
- Are leadership capabilities distributed or concentrated?

Leadership Multiplication: Building Leaders Who Build Leaders

The ultimate measure of presence-driven leadership isn't the results you achieve directly. It's the leaders you develop who go on to achieve results long after you've moved on. Leaders who build leaders multiply their impact exponentially, creating ripple effects that extend far beyond their immediate sphere of influence.

This concept connects directly to everything we've explored in this book. When you coach team members through challenges rather than solving problems for them, you're building their leadership capacity. When you influence through relationship building and credibility rather than by authority, you're modeling a sustainable approach they can replicate. When you lead with conviction while remaining humble and adaptable, you're demonstrating the balance that effective leaders need.

Consider the golf maintenance team story from Chapter 6. By choosing authenticity and accountability over defensiveness, I didn't just solve an immediate relationship problem. I demonstrated to that team what responsive leadership looks like. One of those team members went on to a supervisory role where he applied a similar approach when facing his own leadership challenges.

The New Jersey unionization situation illustrates this principle as well. By investing genuine care and support in one employee during a difficult time, I was modeling the kind of leadership that values people over politics. That approach influenced how other managers on the property began engaging with their teams, creating a culture shift that lasted years beyond my tenure.

Building Leadership Capacity Throughout the Organization

The Coach-Influence-Conviction framework naturally develops leadership capabilities in others:

Coaching develops coaching: When you consistently ask powerful questions and help people think through challenges, they begin using the same approach with their peers and direct reports.

Influence develops influence: When people experience authentic relationship-building and principled persuasion, they learn to build their own credibility and influence networks.

Conviction develops conviction: When team members see leaders making values-based decisions consistently, they gain confidence to stand on their own principles when situations demand it.

The key is being intentional about this development. Every interaction becomes an opportunity to model the leadership behaviors you want to see replicated throughout the organization. This requires patience because leadership development takes time but the long-term impact is transformational.

Leadership multiplication isn't about creating followers who do exactly what you would do. It's about developing leaders who apply presence-driven principles in their own authentic way, adapted to their unique strengths and situations. The frameworks remain consistent but the individual expression varies based on personality, role, and context.

30-Day Implementation Plan

Rather than trying to implement everything at once, use this structured approach to build presence-driven leadership capabilities systematically.

Week 1: Foundation Building
- Complete the integrated self-assessment.
- Choose one area for primary focus.
- Begin daily reflection practice (5 minutes per day).
- Identify three key relationships to strengthen.

Week 2: Coaching Focus
- Practice the five-minute coach check before meetings.
- Have at least three coaching conversations instead of directive interactions.
- Ask more questions and give fewer answers.
- Notice when you jump to solutions versus helping others think through problems.

Week 3: Influence Building
- Conduct weekly influence inventory
- Reach out to support someone who isn't asking for help
- Share valuable information or resources with colleagues
- Focus on building credibility through competence and character

Week 4: Conviction Practice
- Use the values decision filter for all significant choices
- Have one difficult conversation you've been avoiding
- Make one decision based on long-term values rather than short-term convenience
- Share a story about how values guided a past decision

Month 2 and Beyond:
- Continue daily reflection practice
- Rotate monthly focus areas (coaching, influence, conviction)
- Track cultural health indicators relevant to your role
- Look for opportunities to develop leadership capabilities in others

The goal of this implementation plan isn't to add more tasks to your schedule. It's to help you approach your existing responsibilities with greater intentionality and impact. Presence-driven leadership becomes sustainable when it's integrated into how you naturally work rather than layered on top of everything else.

Start small: Choose one or two practices that feel most natural and build from there.

Be consistent: Daily five-minute practices create more impact than occasional hour-long sessions.

Focus on relationships: Every framework in this book works better when applied within strong relational foundations.

Measure what matters: Track cultural health and leadership development, not just traditional performance metrics.

Stay patient: Leadership development takes time, both for yourself and others.

Learn continuously: Use every interaction as data about what works and what doesn't in your specific context.

Remember, presence-driven leadership isn't about perfection—it's about progression. Each day offers new opportunities to show up with greater authenticity, to coach rather than control, to influence through service, and to lead with conviction while remaining humble and adaptable. Your team is waiting for this kind of leadership, and you have the capacity to provide it, starting today, regardless of your title or formal authority.

The journey of presence-driven leadership never ends but the impact begins the moment you choose to lead from who you are rather than what you're called. That choice is always available to you, in every interaction, every decision, and every opportunity to serve others through your leadership. Your presence is your power. Use it wisely.

CHAPTER 11

Being a Presence-Driven Leader

The photograph on the wall that sits over my shoulder tells a story that spans nearly a century of leadership. Three men who never held executive titles, never attended leadership seminars, and never read business books, yet each understood something fundamental about influence and impact. They knew that leadership flows from who you are, not what you're called.

Bill Simmons, the moonshining sharecropper who taught hard work and entrepreneurship. Willie Fate Simmons, who worked three jobs with dignity and treated every person with respect. Lee Simmons, who made history on Air Force One through humility and service. Each passed down the same core truth: presence, not position, creates lasting influence.

That legacy shaped my understanding of leadership long before I had any formal authority. It guided me through every role from front desk agent to corporate vice president. And it forms the foundation of everything we've explored in this book.

We began by establishing that presence-driven leadership isn't about perfection or having all the answers. It's about leading from authenticity, developing others through coaching, building influence through relationships, and making decisions guided by clear values.

We explored the inner work that makes everything else possible. Self-awareness isn't optional for effective leadership. You cannot coach others effectively if you don't understand your own triggers and blind spots. You cannot influence with integrity if you're not clear about your own motivations. You cannot lead with conviction if you haven't clarified your core values.

We discovered that coaching through challenges builds people while solving problems. Every difficult conversation becomes an opportunity for development when you ask questions instead of providing answers, when you help people think through solutions instead of thinking for them.

We learned that influence without authority is not only possible but essential in today's workplace. Building credibility through competence and character, understanding what motivates others, and aligning your requests with their interests creates sustainable influence that outlasts any formal role.

We examined how leading with conviction provides direction while maintaining the humility and adaptability that keeps you effective. Your values become your compass, guiding decisions when everything else is uncertain, while remaining open to new information and different approaches.

Through real-world stories, we saw how these principles work together in complex situations. The golf maintenance team taught us that authenticity builds trust faster than perfection. The New Jersey experience showed us that genuine care for individuals can transform entire cultures. The Diversity, Equity, & Inclusion crisis demonstrated that conviction-driven leadership can navigate controversy while building something stronger.

We explored how to build team culture without formal authority, how to lead through crisis and change, and how to adapt presence-driven principles to modern workplace challenges. Throughout it all, the core message remained consistent: leadership is about who you are and how you show up, not what your title says you should be able to do.

The Coach-Influence-Conviction framework isn't three separate skills you develop in isolation. They work together as an integrated approach to leadership that serves others while achieving results.

When you coach effectively, you build the relationships that enhance your influence. When you influence with integrity, you build the trust that enables deeper coaching conversations. When you lead with conviction, you model the authenticity that makes both coaching and influence more powerful.

This integration creates a reinforcing cycle. The more you develop others, the more influence you gain. The more influence you build, the more opportunities you have to coach and develop people. The more clearly you live your values, the more others trust your coaching and respect your influence.

But the framework only works when it's grounded in genuine care for others' success. Coaching becomes manipulation if it's about getting people to do what you want rather than helping them grow. Influence becomes exploitation if it's about advancing your agenda rather than serving shared interests. Conviction becomes stubbornness if it's about being right rather than doing right.

The difference is your intention. Presence-driven leaders use these capabilities to serve others and achieve outcomes that benefit everyone involved. That's what transforms techniques into genuine leadership.

Every choice you make as a leader creates ripples that extend far beyond what you can see. When you choose to coach someone through a challenge instead of solving it for them, you're not just addressing that immediate situation. You're modeling a leadership approach they may use with others for years to come.

When you build influence through authentic relationships and consistent character, you're not just creating your own network of support. You're demonstrating how trust is built and maintained in professional relationships.

When you make decisions based on clear values, especially when it's difficult or costly, you're not just solving today's problem. You're showing others what principled leadership looks like and giving them permission to stand on their own convictions when faced with similar choices.

This ripple effect is how presence-driven leadership multiplies impact. You don't just achieve results through your own actions. You develop other leaders who achieve results through their actions and develop other leaders in return, creating expanding circles of influence that can transform entire organizations and communities.

Think about the leaders who influenced your own development the most. Chances are, they didn't just teach you what to do. They showed you who to be. They modeled the kind of leadership that inspired you to develop your own capabilities and extend that influence to others.

That's the opportunity you have now. Every interaction is a chance to model presence-driven leadership. Every coaching conversation is an opportunity to develop someone's capabilities. Every relationship you build creates potential for positive influence. Every values-based decision you make demonstrates what principled leadership looks like.

The principles in this book aren't theoretical concepts to discuss in leadership meetings. They're practical approaches you can begin implementing immediately, regardless of your current role or level of formal authority.

You don't need permission to start coaching people through challenges instead of solving problems for them. You don't need approval to begin building influence through authentic relationships and consistent character. You don't need a promotion to start making decisions based on clear values.

Presence-driven leadership begins with a choice: Will you lead from who you are or from what you're called? Will you focus on developing others or just getting things done? Will you build influence through service or seek power through position? Will you make decisions based on your values or your convenience?

These choices are available to you in every interaction, every conversation, and every decision you face. The front desk agent who builds relationships across departments is practicing presence-driven leadership. The middle manager who coaches team members through challenges instead of micromanaging their work is demonstrating these principles. The senior executive who makes difficult decisions based on clear values is living this approach.

Your title might change throughout your career. Your responsibilities will certainly evolve. The organizations you work for will likely shift their strategies and structures. But your capacity for presence-driven leadership travels with you wherever you go.

Start today by choosing one person to coach rather than direct. Instead of telling them what to do, ask questions that help them think through the situation and develop their own solutions. Build one authentic relationship by reaching out to someone who could benefit from your support or expertise, without expecting anything in return.

Make one decision based on your values. When faced with a choice today, ask yourself what decision aligns with your core principles rather than what's most convenient or popular.

These small actions won't transform your organization overnight. But they will begin to transform you as a leader. And as you change, the people around you will begin to change. That's how sustainable leadership development happens. One choice, one conversation, one relationship at a time.

In a world of constant change, competing priorities, and complex challenges, your values provide the only reliable guidance for leadership decisions. When you're clear about what you stand for, you can navigate uncertainty with confidence. When others see you consistently living your principles, they learn to trust your judgment even when they don't fully understand your reasoning.

Your conviction isn't about being rigid or unwilling to consider other perspectives. It's about having a moral and ethical compass that guides your decisions while remaining open to new information and different approaches. It's about knowing what you won't compromise while staying flexible about how you achieve your goals.

This compass becomes especially important during crisis, conflict, and change. When everything around you is shifting, your values provide stability. When pressure mounts to compromise your principles, your conviction gives you the strength to do what's right rather than what's easy.

The leaders who create lasting positive change are those who remain grounded in their values while adapting their methods to serve others effectively. They understand that leadership is ultimately about service by helping others succeed, developing capabilities throughout the organization, and creating environments where people can do their best work.

Every day you lead, you're writing a story that others will remember long after your formal role has ended. The question is: What kind of story will it be?

Will it be a story about someone who used their position to advance their own interests, or someone who used their influence to serve others? Will it be about someone who hoarded power and information, or someone who developed capabilities throughout the organization? Will it be about someone who made decisions based on convenience and politics, or someone who consistently chose values over expediency?

The story you write through your leadership creates the legacy you leave behind. That legacy isn't measured by the titles you held or the budgets you managed. It's measured by the people you developed, the culture you created, and the principles you demonstrated through your choices.

Some of the most impactful leaders I've known never held the highest positions in their organizations. But they influenced countless people through their presence, their character, and their commitment to serving others. They understood that leadership is not about the power you accumulate but the power you give away through developing others.

You have the opportunity to write that kind of leadership story. Starting today, in your current role, with your existing responsibilities, you can choose to lead with presence rather than position. You can choose to develop others rather than just direct them. You can choose to influence through service rather than authority.

Your people are waiting for this kind of leadership. They want to be developed, not just managed. They want to be influenced toward shared goals, not just controlled through authority. They want to be led by someone with clear values, not just clear directives.

The world needs leaders who understand that lasting influence comes from character, not position. Organizations need leaders who build cultures of growth, trust, and values-driven decision-making. Communities need leaders who serve others while achieving results that benefit everyone involved.

You can be that kind of leader. You already have everything you need: the capacity for self-awareness, the ability to ask coaching questions, the opportunity to build authentic relationships, and the values that can guide your decisions.

Your conviction is your compass. Trust it. Follow it. Let it guide you toward the kind of leadership that creates positive change wherever you go. The journey of presence-driven leadership never ends, but the impact begins the moment you choose to lead from who you are rather than what you're called. That choice is always available to you. Make it today.

ACKNOWLEDGMENTS

This book stands on the shoulders of three generations of leaders who taught me that presence, not position, creates lasting influence. My great-grandfather, Bill Simmons, worked the fields as a sharecropper in Conecuh County, Alabama, by day and turned his grit into entrepreneurship by night, building one of the most well-known moonshining operations in the county. That "side hustle" wasn't about notoriety, it was about survival, about providing for his family when the odds were stacked high. Bill taught resilience, ingenuity, and the courage to take risks when there were no easy paths forward.

My grandfather, Willie Fate Simmons, didn't wait for opportunity to knock; he created it. He worked three jobs for over thirty years: a cook in the Navy Reserve, head maître d' at Firestone's executive lounge, and a waiter at the Mayflower Hotel. When he was done working for others, he built a successful catering business of his own. On less than an eighth-grade education, he taught himself French and Spanish from old records and ended up serving executives, socialites, and community leaders all across Akron, Ohio. Willie showed me that excellence isn't about what's written on your résumé. It's about how you show up, treat people, and create your own legacy.

My father, Lee F. Simmons, started out on the same Alabama farm, working day in and day out until he went into the service and went on to make history as the first Black steward on Air Force One. Dad served U.S. Presidents from Johnson through Ford with humility, professionalism, and quiet strength. When President Ford lost his reelection, he was so moved by my father's presence that he invited him to join his staff as Special Assistant. To me, Dad's legacy was about servant leadership; about showing up with integrity, consistency, and purpose no matter the stage.

As their great-grandson, grandson, and son, I carry that baton. This book is my contribution to the same lineage: helping leaders not just lead teams but build other leaders, because that is how true legacies are made.

My deepest gratitude goes to the leaders who shaped my understanding of what presence-driven leadership looks like in practice:

Ingeborg Vorderwinkler gave me my first shot as a leader in Housekeeping as an inspector and night supervisor. Inge showed me how to be meticulous with the details, to be punctual, how to be tough when someone is out of step yet show kindness when it was least expected.

Sam Garcia, whom I call the Yoda of being a boss, showed me how to listen and put team members at ease, how to figure out something on your own with what seemed to be his mind, the importance of continual learning, and how to stretch your scope of work to get the next opportunity.

Tim Sullivan showed me how to be a consummate leader, demonstrating the power of leading with influence rather than authority alone. He was also a fantastic orator, and I learned from how he did it with such poise and ease.

Susana Wolfe taught me everything I know and practice to be a successful HR leader. Her guidance became the foundation of my approach to people leadership.

Frank Garahan gave me my first shot as a first-time Executive Committee member as Director of Human Resources. He showed me how to build relationships with team members as a senior leader, how to lead by walking around, and how to prepare for owner visits with the attention and respect they deserved.

Louis Roden paved the way for my ability to handle multiple properties and showed me what courage and conviction look like when leadership gets difficult.

Ken Pilgrim taught me true servant leadership at all levels of the organization, demonstrating that leadership is about service, not self-advancement.

Special thanks to Bruce Jordan, who would not let up on suggesting I write a book and challenged me not to write just one but three books! Know that this is one of seven currently in development. Thanks, Bruce, for pushing me to share what I've learned.

To my writing coach, whose guidance and expertise helped transform years of leadership experience into the structured framework and practical tools that fill these pages.

Today, as I complete this book, I stand alongside my wife, Kenia, who has been everything through every transition, and my first and forever fans: my sisters Donica and Rona, my brother Ottoway, and my children—Victor, Michelle, and Roman. They remind me daily why this work matters and why leadership is not about authority—it's about legacy.

With deep gratitude to my personal "board of directors," past and present—those trusted advisors and friends who challenge my thinking, hold me accountable, and remind me that no leader truly goes it alone.

Finally, to every team member I've had the privilege to lead and every leader I've had the opportunity to coach: you have taught me as much as I've taught you. This book exists because of the real-world laboratory of leadership we created together.

To the readers who will take these principles and adapt them to your own leadership journey: thank you for the trust you place in these ideas and for the impact you will create through your own presence-driven leadership.

ABOUT THE AUTHOR

Victor Simmons is a global HR executive, DEIB strategist, and founder of Victorious Endeavors, a coaching, consulting, and speaking firm dedicated to building inclusive, people-centered workplaces where leaders thrive and teams deliver.

With more than 20 years of leadership experience, Victor has led HR operations and cultural transformation across the U.S., Canada, Japan, Australia, and Greece. He has served in leadership roles with global hospitality brands including La Quinta Resort & Club, Marriott International, Starwood Hotels, Wyndham Hotels & Resorts, and most recently as Vice President of Human Resources for Atelier Ace, where he guided organizational strategy, employee engagement, and diversity initiatives at scale.

Victor's career has been shaped by both resilience and reinvention. From starting as a dishwasher to rising through conference services, operations, and human resources leadership, he has consistently turned challenges into opportunities for growth. His experience navigating industry downturns, leading through crisis, and building cultures of accountability and care reflects the very principles he teaches in this book: presence-driven leadership, authentic influence, and the power of developing others.

A sought-after speaker and trainer, Victor is recognized for his practical, inspiring approach to leadership development, workplace culture, and DEIB strategy. His thought leadership has been featured on panels, podcasts, and conferences, where he equips audiences with actionable tools to lead in today's rapidly evolving workplace. He is known for his signature frameworks, including Coach-Influence-Conviction, and his philosophy that "presence, not position" creates lasting leadership impact.

Beyond his professional work, Victor draws strength from his family, his wife Kenia, and his children Victor, Michelle, and Roman, and the legacy of his paternal ancestors: Bill Simmons, whose entrepreneurial spirit and resilience; Willie Fate Simmons, whose work ethic and relationship-building excellence; and Lee F. Simmons, the first Black steward on Air Force One, whose servant leadership and quiet strength continue to guide Victor's leadership philosophy.

The Presence-Driven Leader represents the culmination of Victor's experience leading diverse teams, navigating organizational change, and coaching leaders at all levels to develop their authentic leadership presence. Through this book, he continues his mission to help leaders create positive change by focusing on who they are rather than what they're called.

Connect with Victor:
- Website: https://www.victoriousendeavors-consulting.com/
- LinkedIn: https://www.linkedin.com/in/victorsimmons/

GLOSSARY

CLEAR Framework: A crisis communication model using (C)ommunicate frequently, (L)isten actively, (E) what you know, (A)cknowledge emotions, and (R)einforce values and priorities.

Coach-Influence-Conviction Framework: The three-pillar foundation of presence-driven leadership: coaching through challenges to develop people, influencing without authority through relationships and credibility, and leading with conviction based on clear values.

Coaching Through Challenges: Helping people develop problem-solving capabilities by asking questions and providing guidance rather than providing immediate solutions or taking over tasks.

Conviction-Based Leadership: Making decisions guided by clear personal values and principles, especially during difficult situations, while remaining open to new information and approaches.

Emotional Intelligence: The ability to recognize, understand, and manage your own emotions while effectively recognizing and responding to others' emotions. Includes self-awareness, self-management, social awareness, and relationship management.

GROW Model: A coaching conversation framework using Goal (what are we trying to achieve), Reality (what's the current situation), Options (what possibilities exist), and Way Forward (what specific actions will we take).

Influence Without Authority: The ability to drive outcomes and create change through credibility, relationships, and persuasion rather than relying on formal position or hierarchical power.

Leadership Multiplication: The practice of developing other leaders who go on to develop additional leaders, creating expanding circles of leadership capability throughout an organization.

Motivation Conversation Framework: A three-question approach for understanding team members: What do they want? What do you see? What do they need to hear right now?

Positional Leadership: A leadership approach that relies primarily on formal authority, hierarchy, and organizational power to direct others and achieve results.

Presence-Driven Leadership: Leading through authentic character, genuine relationships, and consistent values rather than relying on formal authority or position. Emphasizes who you are over what you're called.

Psychological Safety: The belief that you can speak up, ask questions, make mistakes, and be vulnerable without fear of negative consequences to your career, status, or relationships.

Self-Awareness: Understanding your own emotions, triggers, values, strengths, weaknesses, and impact on others. The foundation for effective leadership development.

Servant Leadership: A leadership philosophy that prioritizes serving others and helping them grow and succeed rather than accumulating power or advancing personal interests.

The Five Traits: Key characteristics that next-generation teams respond to: Clarity, Consistency (caring + connected + communication), Coaching (not commanding), Flexibility (scheduling + work duties), and Purpose (performance expectations + how role adds value).

Values-based Decision Making: Using clearly defined personal principles and ethics as the primary guide for choices, especially when facing difficult situations or competing priorities.

RESOURCES AND REFERENCES

This book draws from research, leadership frameworks, and real-world experience to provide practical tools for presence-driven leadership. The following resources informed key concepts and provided supporting evidence for the principles discussed throughout the book.

Key Research and Studies

Emotional Intelligence and Self-Awareness:
- Eurich, Tasha. Insight: The Surprising Truth About How Others See Us, How We See Ourselves, and Why the Answers Matter More Than We Think. Crown Business, 2017.

Team Effectiveness and Psychological Safety:
- Google's Project Aristotle. Research identifying psychological safety as the most important factor in team effectiveness, more predictive of success than individual talent or team composition.

Leadership Development and Performance:
- Center for Creative Leadership. "How to Influence People: 4 Skills for Influencing Others." CCL, 2025 www.ccl.org/articles/leading-effectively-articles/4-keys-strengthen-ability-influence-others/.

Employee Engagement and Leadership:
- Gallup. Research consistently showing that employee engagement hovers around 30% globally, with the connection between leadership quality and employee engagement being well-documented.

Coaching Culture Impact:
- International Coach Federation. Research showing that organizations with strong coaching cultures report 51% higher employee engagement and 48% higher performance than those without.

Generational Workplace Research

Millennial and Gen Z Workplace Insights:
- Barton, Derrick (Founder) and McKenzie Barton (Life Work Solutions Lead), Center for Talent Solutions. Generational workplace culture research and leadership style preferences data that informed Chapter 9's insights on leading multi-generational teams.

Leadership Frameworks Referenced

GROW Coaching Model:
- A widely used coaching conversation framework utilizing Goal, Reality, Options, and Way Forward components.

Emotional Intelligence Framework:
- Goleman, Daniel. Four-domain model of emotional intelligence, including self-awareness, self-management, social awareness, and relationship management.

Servant Leadership Principles:
- Greenleaf, Robert K. Foundational concepts of servant leadership that emphasize serving others' growth and success.

Additional Influences

Leadership Development Research:
- Various studies on leadership effectiveness, influence without authority, and values-based decision making that support the Coach-Influence-Conviction framework.

Crisis Leadership and Change Management:
- Research on organizational resilience, crisis communication, and leading through uncertainty that informed Chapters 6-8.

Modern Workplace Trends:
- Studies on remote work effectiveness, hybrid team leadership, and digital communication that shaped Chapter 9's guidance on contemporary leadership challenges.

Note: This book is based primarily on practical experience and established leadership principles rather than extensive academic research. The references listed represent key studies and frameworks that validate and support the presence-driven leadership approach described throughout the book.